Series / Number 07-032

MEASURES OF ASSOCIATION

ALBERT M. LIEBETRAU
Battelle Pacific Northwest Laboratories
Richland, Washington

SAGE PUBLICATIONS
The International Professional Publishers
Newbury Park   London   New Delhi

For information address:

SAGE Publications, Inc.
2455 Teller Road
Newbury Park, California 91320
E-mail: order@sagepub.com

SAGE Publications Ltd.
6 Bonhill Street
London EC2A 4PU
United Kingdom

SAGE Publications India Pvt. Ltd.
M-32 Market
Greater Kailash I
New Delhi 110 048 India

Printed in the United States of America

International Standard Book Number 0-8037-1974-3

Library of Congress Catalog Card No. L.C. 83-60229

96 97 98 99 00 01 15 14 13 12 11 10

When citing a university paper, please use the proper form. Remember to cite the Sage University Paper series title and include the paper number. One of the following formats can be adapted (depending on the style manual used):

(1) LIEBETRAU, ALBERT M. (1983) Measures of association. Sage University Paper Series on Quantitative Applications in the Social Sciences, 07-032. Newbury Park, CA: Sage.

OR

(2) Liebetrau, A. M. (1983). *Measures of association* (Sage University Paper Series on Quantitative Applications in the Social Sciences, series no. 07-032). Newbury Park, CA: Sage.

CONTENTS

Series Editor's Introduction

Disciplines such as political science, psychology, and sociology have all been moving in the direction of multivariate, regression-based analysis. Yet research questions—especially in the initial stages—are often based on the relationship among a small set of variables, where the principal concern is with the strength of the links between the variables. Likewise, distinctions between various levels of measurement are being less sharply adhered to than in the past. Yet a concern over differences in types of and precision of measurement is still of genuine interest. Theoretically, a linear relationship is most often assumed. Yet interest remains in just what kind of relationship is "perfect." For all of these reasons, *Measures of Association* by Albert Liebetrau is an appropriate addition to our series.

Liebetrau's work is thorough but readable. The reader will find the basic equations for a large number of the most widely used statistics along with examples that clarify computations that are occasionally complex. Additionally, relationships among the various measures are specified, and advantages and disadvantages of specific statistics or classes of statistics are identified.

The author pays particular attention to the sampling distributions necessary to determine levels of significance and confidence intervals. The formulas necessary to derive these distributions are typically more complex than are the formulas for the statistics themselves. This makes the monograph slightly more complicated than it would otherwise be, but it adds considerably to the value for someone interested in seriously understanding and using the measures described. Basic knowledge of elementary statistics is required to make the best use of this material.

—*Richard G. Niemi*
Series Co-Editor

MEASURES OF ASSOCIATION

ALBERT M. LIEBETRAU
Battelle Pacific Northwest Laboratories
Richland, Washington

1. INTRODUCTION

Much human endeavor is devoted to the discovery of important relationships, or *associations*. It is seldom enough to know only that some relationship exists, so research is usually undertaken to quantify the association. The ultimate goal may be to establish a cause-effect relationship, but quantification is often the first step toward achieving that goal.

This monograph focuses on measures of association between two attributes, or *variables*. Roughly speaking, two variables are associated if they are not independent. Two variables are said to be *independent* if changes in the value of one have no effect on the value of the other.

I begin by discussing some basic statistical ideas. Whatever the objective, an important first step is to identify an appropriate *population*. The population may be quite explicitly defined (the voting population of the United States, for example), or it may be more conceptual in nature (the target population of an advertising campaign to introduce a new soft drink). There are many situations in which members of a population can be quite difficult to identify (people with emotional characteristics that make them especially susceptible to hypertension).

Suppose that we can observe two variables for the members of some population. It is customary to denote the variables by capital letters, such as X and Y. An example is instructive: Consider all the high school seniors who have taken Scholastic Aptitude Tests (SATs) within the past year (the population), and let X and Y denote math and verbal scores, respectively. It is natural to ask how X and Y are related. As a second example, suppose we are interested in the relationship between education and income. For a population of individuals in the 40 to 60 age range, let X denote the number of years of formal education and let Y be current annual income.

It would be ideal if values of X and Y could be observed for each member of the population. This is seldom practical and often impossible; usually one must settle for observations on some subset of the population. The subset selected is called a *sample*, and the method of selection is called a *sampling plan*. It is convenient to let $(X_1, Y_1), \ldots, (X_n, Y_n)$ denote the values of X and Y, called *observations*, for a sample of n members of the population.

A sample may be selected purely for convenience, but a more formal sampling plan is preferable. In this monograph, I will nearly always assume that sampling is random. A *random sample* is one in which each member of the population has the same chance of being selected in the sample as does any other member of the population.

Statisticians distinguish between *descriptive* and *inferential* methods. When all members of the population are sampled, then we know everything there is to know about X and Y, both individually and jointly, for that population. We need only to *describe* the results in some meaningful and concise way; hence, the term "descriptive statistics."

If the sample is a subset of the population, the sample values of (X, Y) are only one of many possible sets that might have been observed. Here one must use the sample values to *infer* properties of the entire population. Valid inferences depend on knowledge of the way in which observed values vary from sample to sample, that is, on the *sampling distribution* of the variables of interest. The sampling distribution, in turn, depends on both the sampling plan and the nature of the variables themselves. Strictly speaking, inferential methods apply only to data obtained by some systematic, well-defined sampling plan, such as random sampling. In particular, they are not applicable to data acquired by "convenience sampling."

Random variables are classified as continuous or discrete according to the set of possible values they can assume. Discrete variables are further classified as nominal, ordinal, or scalar. As might be expected, proper methods of statistical inference differ from class to class.

Variables that can at least theoretically assume all possible values in some interval are called *continuous* or *interval* variables. *Discrete* variables are those for which the set of all possible values is some discrete set of numbers. Since discrete variables often identify categories into which population members fall, they are also called *categorical* variables.

An example will prove helpful. If "family income" is recorded for a sample of families to the degree of accuracy required by the Internal Revenue Service, this variable can be regarded as continuous. For many purposes, it suffices to classify families into broad income categories. When income is expressed in thousands of dollars, one possible classification consists of the categories 0-5, 5-10, 10-25, 25-50, and 50+. On this scale, "family income" is a discrete, or categorical, variable.

The class of discrete variables is divided into three subclasses: scalar, ordinal, and nominal. *Nominal* variables are those whose values serve only to identify categories. Values of a nominal variable (i.e., category labels) have no meaningful quantitative relationship to each other. "Sex" is an example of a nominal variable. The two categories can be identified by "M" and "F," or by "1" and "2," or by one of infinitely many other possibilities. The assignment 1 = Male and 2 = Female is equally as valid as the reverse assignment. Since the pairing of category names is quite arbitrary, no meaning can be derived from the fact that one category label is greater than the other.

Often the categories, or levels, of a discrete variable are ordered. When category labels are chosen to identify this order, the resulting variable is called *ordinal*. Ordinal and nominal variables are distinguished by the fact that categories of an ordinal variable are meaningfully ordered, while those of a nominal variable are not.

If the five categories of "family income" defined above are labeled 1, 2, 3, 4, and 5, respectively, "family income" is ordinal. Incomes of families in category 1 are less than incomes of families in other categories, incomes of families in category 4 are greater than incomes of families in category 3 and less than those of families in category 5, and so on.

The following attitude scale is another example of an ordinal variable. Consider the statement: "The United States should increase efforts to develop nuclear energy," where the interviewee is allowed one of five possible responses: (1) strongly agree, (2) agree, (3) no opinion, (4) disagree, or (5) strongly disagree. These responses are clearly ordered.

Category labels of ordinal variables tell us the order of categories, but do not allow the categories to be compared *quantitatively*. An "A" student has scored higher than a "B" student, but we cannot say *how much* higher. Families in category 5 have greater incomes than do those in category 2, but we cannot say that families in category 5 have 2.5 times the income of families in category 2. Discrete variables whose values carry quantitative information (such variables are necessarily ordinal) are called *scalar*, or ratio, variables. "Family income" can be made into a scalar variable by the assignment of "average" or "typical" values to each income category. We could, for example, assign the values 2.5, 7.5, 17.5, 37.5, and 60, respectively, to the five income categories.

Of the three classes of discrete variables, nominal variables are least like continuous variables, and scalar variables are most like continuous variables. It can be difficult to correctly classify a variable, especially if it is created from another variable as in some of the above examples. Nevertheless, it is important that variables be correctly classified if we hope to choose the most informative possible measure of association.

Ordinal and scalar variables arise in two ways: (1) directly from discrete ordinal scales, and (2) indirectly from partitioning the range of some continuous variable into categories. The scale of attitudes concerning increased use of nuclear energy is inherently ordinal, and cannot be made into a scalar variable by reassigning category labels. When a continuous scale is categorized, information is lost—the smaller the number of categories, the greater the loss of information. For this reason, categorical data should be used with caution to make inferences about an underlying continuous variable.

2. SAMPLING DISTRIBUTIONS FOR DISCRETE DATA

Under suitable assumptions, the multinomial distribution is the correct model for random samples from discrete populations. Consequently, this distribution and a special case, the binomial distribution, are fundamental to any discussion of measures of association for discrete data.

The Binomial and Multinomial Distributions

Suppose the members of a population are partitioned into k categories $C_1, \ldots, C_k$ on the basis of some discrete random variable. Let $X_1, X_2, \ldots, X_k$ be the numbers of members in a random sample of size n that are observed to fall into categories $C_1, C_2, \ldots, C_k$, respectively. Provided the population is large enough relative to n, the multinomial distribution is the correct sampling model for $X_1, X_2, \ldots, X_k$.[1]

The sum of the X_is is necessarily equal to the sample size; that is,

$$\sum_{i=1}^{k} X_i = n$$

Since one of the X_is can be determined from the others, it is sometimes convenient to work with a reduced set containing only k − 1 of the X_is.

The case in which k = 2 is not only simple, but also quite important. Suppose that a population is partitioned into two categories, C_1 and C_2. Let X_1 be the number of members in a sample of size n that fall into C_1 (for the reason cited above, $X_2 = n - X_1$ can be ignored). The variable X_1 is called a *binomial random variable*, or X_1 is said to have a *binomial distribution*. Further, if the proportion of the population in C_1 is denoted by p_1, then X_1 is said to have a binomial distribution with parameters n and p_1. The binomial distribution has been extensively tabulated, and a discussion of its properties can be found in any good elementary statistics text. Those that are important to this monograph are summarized below.

If X_1 is a binomial random variable with parameters n and p_1, X_1 has expected value (or mean) $E(X_1) = np_1$ and variance $V(X_1) = np_1(1 - p_1)$.

A version of the famous Central Limit Theorem asserts that for large n, the random variable

$$Z = \frac{X_1 - E(X_1)}{\sqrt{V(X_1)}} = \frac{X_1 - np_1}{\sqrt{np_1(1 - p_1)}}$$

has approximately the distribution of a standard normal random variable. This means that approximate percentage points of the binomial distribution can be computed from tables of the standard normal distribution, provided n is large enough. In practice, the farther p_1 is from 0.5, the larger the sample size must be for the approximation to be adequate. As a rule of thumb, it is probably safe to use the normal approximation if p_1 is between 0.2 and 0.8 and n_1 exceeds 30.[2]

When the proportion p_1 of population members falling into one of two categories is unknown, the population is sampled so that p_1 can be estimated. An obvious estimator is the proportion of members of the sample that fall into category C_1. In symbols, $\hat{p}_1 = X_1/n$, where "$\cdot$" means "is an estimator of." In addition to being intuitively reasonable, p_1 also turns out to be a good estimator of p_1 on theoretical grounds.

Suppose now that the population is partitioned into more than two categories. If sampling is random and the population is large enough relative to sample size, the vector of random variables $(X_1, \ldots, X_k)$, or $(X_1, \ldots, X_{k-1})$, has a *multinomial distribution*. If the proportions of the population in categories $C_1, C_2, \ldots, C_k$ are denoted by $p_1, p_2, \ldots, p_k$, respectively, where $p_i \geqslant 0$ and

$$\sum_{i=1}^{k} p_i = 1$$

then $(X_1, \ldots, X_k)$ is said to have a multinomial distribution with parameters n and $p_1, p_2, \ldots, p_k$. The multinomial probability function specifies the probability of the event $(X_1 = n_1, X_2 = n_2, \ldots, X_k = n_k)$ for all k-tuples of nonnegative integers $(n_1, n_2, \ldots, n_k)$ for which

$$\sum_{i=1}^{k} n_i = n$$

Because it involves so many parameters, the multinomial distribution is seldom tabulated.

Marginally, or by itself, each X_i in the multinomial vector is a binomial random variable. In particular, this means that $E(X_i) = np_i$ and $V(X_i) = np_i(1 - p_i)$. Moreover, for large samples the random variables $Z_i = (X_i - np_i)/\sqrt{np_i(1 - p_i)}$ are approximately distributed as standard normal variables. Estimates of the unknown probabilities p_i can be obtained exactly as in the binomial case: A good estimate of p_i is $p_i = X_i/n$, the proportion of sample values that fall into category C_i. The binomial distribution can be regarded as a special case of the multinomial distribution, or conversely, the multinomial distribution can be regarded as a generalization of the binomial distribution. Both viewpoints will prove convenient from time to time.

Contingency Tables

Tables provide a convenient way to present discrete data, especially if the number of categories is less than the sample size. Table 2 in the next chapter is an example of a *two-way contingency table*. This table gives the joint classification of 3077 "witch hunts" with respect to two variables, the type of institution responsible for the witch hunt and the type of political party system of the country in which the hunt occurred. Classifications with respect to more than two variables produce multiway tables, with the number of dimensions being equal to the number of variables involved.

Note that the row totals in Table 2 are a classification according to type of institution and that column totals are a classification according to type of political system. Column totals are obtained by summing over levels of the row variable (type of institutions), and row totals are gotten by summing over levels of the column variable. Contingency tables obtained by summing over the levels of one or more variables of a higher-dimensional table are called *marginal* tables. In other words, a marginal table results from *collapsing* a higher-way table.

In this monograph, I will deal exclusively with two-way contingency tables and corresponding one-way marginal tables. Table 1 shows the terminology that will be employed for an $I \times J$ table. The row variable X has I levels and the column variable Y has J levels. The number of members of a sample of size n that fall into cell (i, j) of the table is denoted by n_{ij}. Thus, n_{ij} is the number of members in the sample classified at the ith level of X and the jth level of Y. The n_{ij}s can be thought of as the observed values of the multinomial variables N_{ij}.[3]

Marginal tables are obtained by summation. Row totals are obtained by summing over columns, and vice versa. Thus, n_{i+} is the number of members of the sample for which X = i and, similarly, n_{+j} is the number in the sample for which Y = j. It is convenient to write the total sample size $n_{++} = \Sigma_i n_{i+} = \Sigma_j n_{+j}$ without subscripts.

The p's shown in Table 1 have interpretations similiar to those of the corresponding n's, except that the p's denote population probabilities, rather than sample counts. The p_{ij}s are usually unknown in practice.

The probability that an arbitrarily chosen member of the population is classified into cell (i, j) is p_{ij}, so that $E(N_{ij}) = E_{ij} = np_{ij}$ is the number in the sample that can be expected to fall into that cell. Now, sets of values

TABLE 1
Notation for a Two-Way Contingency Table

		1	2	...	J	Totals
				Y		
X	1	n_{11}	n_{12}	...	n_{1J}	n_{1+}
		p_{11}	p_{12}		p_{1J}	p_{1+}
	2	n_{21}	n_{22}	...	n_{2J}	n_{2+}
		p_{21}	p_{22}		p_{2J}	p_{2+}
	...	...	...	...	...	...
	I	n_{I1}	n_{I2}	...	n_{IJ}	n_{I+}
		p_{I1}	p_{I2}		p_{IJ}	p_{I+}
	Totals	n_{+1}	n_{+2}	...	n_{+J}	$n_{++}=n$
		p_{+1}	p_{+2}		p_{+J}	$p_{++}=1$

$\{p_{ij}\}$ can be hypothesized for the population. Statistical methods exist that enable us to decide whether the corresponding *hypothesized* cell frequencies $\{np_{ij}\}$ are consistent with *observed* cell frequencies $\{n_{ij}\}$. One method is based on the chi-square goodness-of-fit statistic, which (in the present context) has the general form

$$X^2 = \sum_{i=1}^{I} \sum_{j=1}^{J} \frac{(n_{ij} - np_{ij})^2}{np_{ij}} \qquad [2.1]$$

In case X and Y are independent, $p_{ij} = p_{i+}p_{+j}$ for each i and j. Substitution of the estimates

$$\hat{p}_{ij} = \hat{p}_{i+}\hat{p}_{+j} = \frac{n_{i+}}{n} \frac{n_{+j}}{n}$$

into equation 2.1 yields

$$X^2 = \sum_{i=1}^{I} \sum_{j=1}^{J} \frac{(n_{ij} - n_{i+}n_{+j}/n)^2}{n_{i+}n_{+j}/n} \qquad [2.2]$$

If X and Y are independent, equation 2.2 has approximately the distribution of a chi-square variable with parameter (degrees of freedom) df = $(I - 1)(J - 1)$. The chi-square statistic can be used to establish association: If X^2 is larger than a suitable percentage point of the appropriate chi-square distribution, then X and Y are not independent.

The chi-square statistic plays an important role in the development of Chapter 3. For future reference, it should be noted that equation 2.2 is algebraically identical to

$$X^2 = \frac{n(n_{11}n_{22} - n_{21}n_{12})^2}{n_{1+}n_{+1}n_{2+}n_{+2}} \qquad [2.3]$$

in the fourfold case $I = J = 2$.

3. MEASURES OF ASSOCIATION FOR NOMINAL DATA

Measures of association for nominal data should not depend on the particular order in which the categories are listed, and all the measures discussed in this chapter share that property. Among the oldest measures for nominal data are those based on the *chi-square statistic*, some of which are described in the next section.

Measures Based on the Chi-Square Statistic

One widely accepted interpretation of "no association" in a two-way contingency table is that row and column variables are independent. The classical test of the hypothesis of independence is based on the chi-square statistic X^2 of equation 2.2. For an $I \times J$ contingency table, let $q = \min\{I, J\}$. It is easy to show that X^2 achieves its maximum value of $n(q - 1)$ when each row (if $I \geqslant J$) or each column (if $I \leqslant J$) of the table contains a single nonzero entry.[4] Clearly, $X^2 \geqslant 0$, so that $0 \leqslant X^2 \leqslant n(q - 1)$.

PEARSON'S COEFFICIENT OF MEAN SQUARE CONTINGENCY

The population analogue of equation 2.2, defined by

$$\phi^2 = \sum_{i=1}^{I} \sum_{j=1}^{J} \frac{(p_{ij} - p_{i+}p_{+j})^2}{p_{i+}p_{+j}} = \sum_{i=1}^{I} \sum_{j=1}^{J} \frac{p_{ij}^2}{p_{i+}p_{+j}} - 1 \qquad [3.1]$$

is called the (Pearson) coefficient of mean square contingency. It follows by the reasoning of the previous paragraph that $0 \leqslant \phi^2 \leqslant q - 1$, with $\phi^2 = 0$ in the case of independence and $\phi^2 = q - 1$ in the case of perfect association. By replacing the p's in equation 3.1 with sample estimates, the estimator $\hat{\phi}^2 = X^2/n$ of ϕ^2 is obtained. Since its range depends on the dimensions of the table, ϕ^2 is not particularly suitable as a measure of association without modification.

PEARSON'S CONTINGENCY COEFFICIENT
AND SAKODA'S MODIFICATION

To overcome this difficulty, Pearson (1948) proposed the measure

$$p = \left(\frac{\phi^2}{1 + \phi^2} \right)^{1/2}$$

which is bounded between 0 and 1. The measure p is called the (Pearson) contingency coefficient. The maximum likelihood estimator of p under the multinomial sampling model is

$$\hat{p} = \left(\frac{X^2/n}{1 + X^2/n} \right)^{1/2} = \left(\frac{X^2}{n + X^2} \right)^{1/2}$$

Since p assumes a maximum value of $\sqrt{[(q-1)/q]}$ in the case of perfect association, the range of p still depends on the dimensions of the table. Various functions of ϕ^2 have been proposed to alleviate this difficulty. Sakoda (1977) suggests

$$p^* = p/p_{max} = \left(\frac{q\phi^2}{(q-1)(1+\phi^2)} \right)^{1/2} \qquad [3.2]$$

Although this measure has not found favor with previous authors, $p^* = 0$ in the case of independence, and $p^* = 1$ in the case of perfect association, both strict and implicit.

TSCHUPROW'S CONTINGENCY COEFFICIENT

Tschuprow (1919) considered

$$t = \left(\frac{\phi^2}{\sqrt{(I-1)(J-1)}} \right)^{1/2} \qquad [3.3]$$

which has a maximum value of $\sqrt[4]{[(q-1)/\max\{I-1, J-1\}]}^{1/4}$ in the case of perfect association. Unless I and J are nearly equal, the range of t is severely restricted. If I = 3 and J = 10, for example, $t_{max} = \sqrt[4]{2/9} = 0.6866$.

CRAMER'S CONTINGENCY COEFFICIENT

Finally, Cramer (1946) proposed the coefficient

$$v = \left(\frac{\phi^2}{q-1} \right)^{1/2} \qquad [3.4]$$

In the case of perfect association, $v = 1$ for all values of I and J, while $v = 0$ in the case of independence. Estimators of p*, t, and v are obtained by replacing ϕ^2 with $\hat{\phi}^2 = X^2/n$ in equations 3.2, 3.3, and 3.4, respectively. The resulting estimators are in fact maximum likelihood estimators under the multinomial sampling model. Each estimator has the same range as its population analogue.

The exact distributions of the estimators of p, p*, t, and v are difficult to obtain, but approximate large-sample distributions are known. In the case of independence ($\phi^2 = 0$), percentage points of the distributions of the various contingency coefficients are easily computed from those of equation 2.2. For example, the approximate significance level of the observed value t_0 of t can be obtained as follows: Since

$$\Pr(\hat{t} \geqslant t_0) = \Pr(\hat{t}^2 \geqslant t_0^2) = \Pr\left[\frac{X^2}{n\sqrt{(I-1)(J-1)}} \geqslant t_0^2\right]$$

$$= \Pr[X^2 \geqslant nt_0^2\sqrt{(I-1)(J-1)}]$$

it is necessary to evaluate only the last probability using tables of the chi-square distribution. Similar probabilistic statements can be made concerning p, p*, and v.

For correlated random variables ($\phi^2 \neq 0$), Bishop, Fienberg, and Holland (1975: 386) give the following formula for the asymptotic variance of $\hat{\phi}^2 = X^2/n$:

$$\sigma_\infty^2(\hat{\phi}^2) = \frac{1}{n}\left\{4\sum_{i=1}^{I}\sum_{j=1}^{J}\frac{p_{ij}^3}{p_{i+}p_{+j}} - 3\sum_{i=1}^{I}\frac{1}{p_{i+}}\left(\sum_{j=1}^{J}\frac{p_{ij}^2}{p_{i+}p_{+j}}\right)^2\right.$$

$$- 3\sum_{j=1}^{J}\frac{1}{p_{+j}}\left(\sum_{i=1}^{I}\frac{p_{ij}^2}{p_{i+}p_{+j}}\right)^2 + 2\sum_{i=1}^{I}\sum_{j=1}^{J}\left[\frac{p_{ij}}{p_{i+}p_{+j}}\right.\times$$

$$\left.\left.\left(\sum_{i'=1}^{I}\frac{p_{i'j}}{p_{i'+}p_{+j}}\right)\left(\sum_{j'=1}^{J}\frac{p_{ij'}}{p_{i+}p_{+j'}}\right)\right]\right\}$$ [3.5]

If the values of p_{ij} are unknown, an estimator $\hat{\sigma}_\infty^2(\hat{\sigma}^2)$ of equation 3.5 can be obtained by replacing p_{ij} with $\hat{p}_{ij} = n_{ij}/n$ throughout.

The asymptotic variances of p, p*, t, and v can be obtained from $\sigma_\infty^2(\hat{\phi}^2)$ by the δ method (see, for example, Bishop et al., 1975: chap. 14). They are (for $\phi^2 \neq 0$):

$$\sigma_\infty^2(\hat{p}) = \sigma_\infty^2(\hat{\phi}^2)/[4\phi^2(1+\phi^2)^3]$$ [3.6]

$$\sigma_\infty^2(\hat{p}*) = \frac{q}{q-1} \quad \sigma_\infty^2(\hat{p}) = \frac{q\sigma_\infty^2(\hat{\phi}^2)}{4(q-1)\,\phi^2(1+\phi^2)^3} \tag{3.7}$$

$$\sigma_\infty^2(\hat{t}) = \sigma_\infty^2(\hat{\phi}^2)/[4\phi^2\sqrt{(I-1)(J-1)}]$$

$$= \sigma_\infty^2(\hat{\phi}^2)/[4t^2(I-1)(J-1)] \tag{3.8}$$

$$\sigma_\infty^2(\hat{v}) = \sigma_\infty^2(\hat{\phi}^2)/[4\phi^2(q-1)]$$

$$= \sigma_\infty^2(\hat{\phi}^2)/[4v^2(q-1)^2] \tag{3.9}$$

Estimators of these variances (equations 3.6-3.9) are obtained by replacing population parameters with their sample analogues and using equation 3.5, with p_{ij} replaced by $\hat{p}_{ij} = n_{ij}/n$, to estimate $\sigma_\infty^2(\hat{\phi}^2)$.

The main difficulty in using measures of association based on the statistic X^2 is that of finding a meaningful interpretation. The measures do not have simple probabilistic interpretations, and, despite the fact that X^2 is generally considered to be a good statistic for testing the hypothesis of independence, there is no concensus among statisticians that it is also a good measure of association. In terms of squared difference between observed and expected frequencies (calculated under the assumption of independence), the measures are useful for comparing several tables, but those whose ranges depend on the dimensions of the table are not really comparable across tables of different sizes. The measures $p*$ and v, at least, can be interpreted as the proportion of maximum variation due to association, or interaction, between the variables. Finally, Kendall and Stuart (1973: chap. 33) have shown that v^2 is the mean square canonical correlation between the row and column variables of the contingency table.

For 2×2 contingency tables, ϕ^2 is identical to the Pearson product-moment correlation coefficient ρ^2. Consequently, properties of either are properties of both in this context.

Major references for properties of measures based upon X^2 are the books by Kendall and Stuart (1973: chap. 33), Bishop et al. (1975: chap. 11), and Goodman and Kruskal (1980).[5] Brief discussions of these measures, including examples, are also given by Reynolds (1977a), Hays (1963), and Conover (1980).

Measures of Proportional Reduction in Predictive Error

The chi-square statistic and related measures are all motivated by attempts to measure a vaguely specified "lack of independence" between two categorical variables. Goodman and Kruskal (1980), however, discuss two measures that have meaningful interpretations in terms of probabilities of misclassification. Each is a measure of the relative usefulness of one variable in improving the ability to predict the classification of members of the population with respect to a second variable.

Let A be a (row) variable with I levels, let B denote a second (column) variable with J levels, let p_{ij} be the probability that a randomly selected member of the population falls into category i of variable A and category j of variable B, and let n_{ij} be the number of individuals in a sample of size n that fall into cell (i, j) of the classification table. The data (or the population probabilities, if they are known) can be used to predict the A category of a randomly selected individual. Moreover, the prediction can be accomplished either (1) without or (2) with knowledge of the individual's B category. The measures considered by Goodman and Kruskal are defined in terms of the reduction in the probability of misclassification resulting from knowledge of the individual's classification for the second variable. Different classification schemes result in different probabilities of error (measures), but the two schemes of Goodman and Kruskal seem most natural.

The Goodman-Kruskal measures of proportional reduction in predictive error treat the variables asymmetrically. They are especially useful, therefore, in situations in which a causal relationship is sought.

THE GOODMAN-KRUSKAL λ

Suppose that the (marginal) distribution of the row variable A is known, and, with only that information, the task is to estimate the A category of an individual selected at random from the population. One reasonable classification rule specifies that the individual be assigned to the category, or row, with the greatest probability. Thus the individual is assigned to the category corresponding to row m of the table for which

$$p_{m+} = \max \left\{ p_{1+}, p_{2+}, \ldots, p_{I+} \right\}$$

This classification rule maximizes the probability of correct classification; the corresponding probability of misclassification is

$$1 - p_{m+} \qquad [3.10]$$

Now, suppose that the individual is known to fall into category j of the column variable B. Application of the above classification rule to the probabilities *in column j* of the table dictates that the individual be assigned to the A category m for which

$$p_{mj} = \max\left\{ p_{1j}, p_{2j}, \ldots, p_{Ij} \right\}$$

so as to maximize the *conditional* probability p_{mj}/p_{+j} of correct classification, given his B classification. The corresponding probability of *conditional* misclassification is $1 - p_{mj}/p_{+j}$ and the *unconditional* probability of error is

$$\sum_{j=1}^{J} P(\text{Error}|B=j)P(B=j) = \sum_{j=1}^{J} (1 - p_{mj}/p_{+j})p_{+j}$$

$$= \sum_{j=1}^{J} (p_{+j} - p_{mj}) = 1 - \sum_{j=1}^{J} p_{mj} \qquad [3.11]$$

The relative reduction in the probability of prediction error is, from equations 3.10 and 3.11,

$$\lambda_{A|B} = \frac{(1 - p_{m+}) - (1 - \sum_j p_{mj})}{1 - p_{m+}} = \frac{\sum_j p_{mj} - p_{m+}}{1 - p_{m+}} \qquad [3.12]$$

In other words, $\lambda_{A|B}$ is the proportion of relative error in predicting an individual's A category that can be eliminated by knowledge of his or her B category.

The measure $\lambda_{A|B}$ can assume values between 0 and 1, inclusive, and is well defined unless all nonzero probabilities of the table are in a single row. If each column of the table contains at most one nonzero entry, the maximum probability in each column is the same as one of the column marginal probabilities. Consequently, knowledge of an individual's B category permits errorless prediction of his or her A category. The corresponding value of equation 3.12 is: $\lambda_{A|B} = 1$. At the other extreme, if all column maxima occur in the same row, $\lambda_{A|B} = 0$; this is the case if A and B are independent. The independence of A and B implies $\lambda_{A|B} = 0$, but the converse need not be true because all column maxima can also occur in a single row even though the variables are not independent. Bishop et al. (1975: 386-389) give an example in which one of two dependent variables is no help in predicting the other. The fact that measures of predictive association can be zero for correlated variables distinguishes them from measures based on the chi-square statistic. Like the chi-square measures, however, $\lambda_{A|B}$ does remain unchanged if any two rows or any two columns of the table are interchanged.

Measures based on X^2 are effective for determining departures from independence, but they treat variables symmetrically. If the goal is to use one variable to improve the predictability of another, asymmetric measures such as $\lambda_{A|B}$ are better. These remarks also apply to other asymmetric measures, such as the Goodman-Kruskal τ and Somers's d.

Situations certainly exist in which it is of interest to use knowledge of A to improve prediction of B. Interchanging the roles of A and B in the derivation of $\lambda_{A|B}$ yields

$$\lambda_{B|A} = \frac{\sum_i p_{im} - p_{+m}}{1 - p_{+m}} \qquad [3.13]$$

as the relative decrease in the probability of error of predicting B gained from knowledge of A. In equation 3.13, p_{+m} is the maximum of the (marginal) probabilities of the B categories, and p_{im} is the maximum of these probabilities for the ith category of A; i.e., p_{im} is the maximum of the probabilities in the ith row of the contingency table.

Both $\lambda_{A|B}$ and $\lambda_{B|A}$ are designed for use in situations in which one of the variables can reasonably be assumed to depend upon the other. For situations in which no natural asymmetry exists, Goodman and Kruskal (1954) propose the measure

$$\lambda = \frac{\lambda_{A|B}(1 - p_{m+}) + \lambda_{B|A}(1 - p_{+m})}{(1 - p_{m+}) + (1 - p_{+m})}$$

$$= \frac{\sum_j p_{mj} + \sum_i p_{im} - p_{m+} - p_{+m}}{2 - p_{m+} - p_{+m}} \qquad [3.14]$$

The measure λ arises from the following somewhat artificial prediction problem: Suppose that half the time the task is to estimate the B category and half the time the task is to estimate the A category of an individual selected at random from the population. Then λ is the reduction in the probability of prediction error resulting from knowledge of the individual's classification on the second variable relative to the probability of error if this information is not available.

The symmetric measure λ is well defined if at least two cells not both in the same row or the same column of the table contain nonzero probabilities. Since λ is a weighted averge of $\lambda_{A|B}$ and $\lambda_{B|A}$, its value must lie between those of the two asymmetric measures. If the table contains at most one nonzero probability in each row and column, $\lambda = 1$. If A and B are independent, $\lambda = 0$, although λ can be zero even if A and B are not independent.

Under the multinomial sampling model, the maximum likelihood estimators of $\lambda_{A|B}$, $\lambda_{B|A}$, and λ are, respectively,

$$\hat{\lambda}_{A|B} = \frac{\sum_j n_{mj} - n_{m+}}{n - n_{m+}}$$ [3.15]

$$\hat{\lambda}_{A|B} = \frac{\sum_i n_{im} - n_{+m}}{n - n_{+m}}$$ [3.16]

and

$$\hat{\lambda} = \frac{\sum_j n_{mj} + \sum_i n_{im} - n_{m+} - n_{+m}}{2n - n_{m+} - n_{+m}}$$ [3.17]

In equations 3.15 through 3.17, the quantities n_{mj}, n_{m+}, and so on are sample analogues of p_{mj}, p_{m+}, and so on. If "probability" is replaced by "observed frequency," statements about the range, minimum, and maximum of equations 3.12, 3.13, and 3.4 apply verbatim to equations 3.15, 3.16, and 3.17, respectively. Whenever any one of the three measures is either 0 or 1, the corresponding estimator has the same value.

The exact sampling distributions of equations 3.15, 3.16, and 3.17 are unknown, but under the multinomial model, all three estimators are approximately normal for large samples. Provided n is sufficiently large, $n_{m+} \neq 1$, and $\lambda_{A|B}$ is not 0 or 1, Goodman and Kruskal (1963) show that $\lambda_{A|B}$ has approximately a normal sampling distribution with mean $\lambda_{A|B}$ and variance

$$\sigma_\infty^2(\hat{\lambda}_{A|B}) = \frac{\left(1 - \sum_j p_{mj}\right)\left(\sum_j p_{mj} + p_{m+} - 2\sum_j^c p_{mj}\right)}{(1 - p_{m+})^3}$$ [3.18]

where $\sum_j^c p_{mj}$ is the sum of all maximum column probabilities that fall in the same row as p_{m+}. The last factor in the numerator of equation 3.18 is the sum of the p_{mj}s that are not in the same row as p_{m+} and the probabilities in the same row as p_{m+} that are not p_{mj}s. The corresponding estimator of equation 3.18 is:

$$\hat{\sigma}_\infty^2(\hat{\lambda}_{A|B}) = \frac{\left(n - \sum_j n_{mj}\right)\left(\sum_j n_{mj} + n_{m+} - 2\sum_j^c n_{mj}\right)}{(n - n_{m+})^3}$$ [3.19]

where $\overset{c}{\underset{}{\Sigma}} n_{mj}$ is the sum of all maximum column frequencies that occur in the same row as n_{m+}. If $n = n_{m+}$, then equation 3.19 is not defined. Moreover, if ties exist among candidates for n_{m+} or n_{mj}, equation 3.19 may not be uniquely defined, since its value depends on the choice of m. A conservative approach is to use the largest estimate obtained by evaluating equation 3.19 for the various choices of n_{m+} and n_{mj}. The estimator $\hat{\lambda}_{A|B}$ itself is uniquely defined even in the case of ties. Example 1 (later in this chapter) will help to clarify the meaning of the terms in equations 3.18 and 3.19.

The asymptotic distribution of $\hat{\lambda}_{A|B}$ may be used to perform significance tests and compute confidence intervals, provided suitable modifications are taken near 0 or 1. If $\hat{\lambda}_{A|B} = 0$ (or 1), Goodman and Kruskal suggest using the degenerate confidence interval 0 (or 1) for $\lambda_{A|B}$. Likewise, the hypothesis $\lambda_{A|B} = 0$ (or $\lambda_{A|B} = 1$) should be rejected unless $\hat{\lambda}_{A|B} = 0$ (or $\hat{\lambda}_{A|B} = 1$). Approximate confidence intervals with computed lower limits less than 0 or upper limits greater than 1 can be suitably truncated.

It follows by symmetry that $\hat{\lambda}_{B|A}$ is asymptotically a normal random variable with mean $\lambda_{B|A}$ and estimated variance

$$\hat{\sigma}_\infty^2(\hat{\lambda}_{B|A}) = \frac{\left(n - \underset{i}{\Sigma} n_{im}\right)\left(\underset{i}{\Sigma} n_{im} + n_{+m} - 2\overset{r}{\underset{i}{\Sigma}} n_{im}\right)}{(n - n_{+m})^3} \qquad [3.20]$$

where $\overset{r}{\underset{i}{\Sigma}} n_{im}$ is the sum of all maximum row frequencies that fall in the same column as n_{+m}. Comments made about $\hat{\lambda}_{A|B}$ apply also to $\hat{\lambda}_{B|A}$.

The sampling distribution of $\hat{\lambda}$ is also asymptotically normal. However, to write an expression for the estimated sampling variance of $\hat{\lambda}$, we need some additional notation. In each of the following, the symbol to the left of the colon denotes the quantity to the right:

n_{im}: maximum value in row i, i = 1, 2, ..., I

n_{mj}: maximum value in column j, j = 1, 2, ..., J

m_c: index of the column that contains the maximum column marginal, denoted n_{+m_c}

m_r: index of the row which contains the maximum row marginal, denoted n_{m_r+}

$\underset{i}{\Sigma} n_{im}$: sum of all row maxima

$\underset{j}{\Sigma} n_{mj}$: sum of all column maxima

$$\sum_{i}^{r} n_{im_c} : \text{sum of row maxima that fall in column } m_c$$

$$\sum_{j}^{c} n_{m_r j} : \text{sum of column maxima that fall in row } m_r$$

$$\sum_{i}^{*} n_{im} : \text{sum of all column (row) maxima that are also row (column) maxima}$$

In addition, let

$$U_1 = \frac{1}{n} \left(n_{+m_c} + n_{m_r +} \right)$$

$$U_2 = \frac{1}{n} \left(\sum_{i} n_{im} + \sum_{j} n_{mj} \right)$$

$$U_3 = \frac{1}{n} \left(\sum_{i}^{r} n_{im_c} + \sum_{j}^{c} n_{m_r j} + n_{m_r m} + n_{mm_c} \right)$$

Provided λ is not equal to 0 or 1, Goodman and Kruskal (1963) show that for large n, $\hat{\lambda}$ is approximately a normal random variable with mean λ and estimated variance

$$\hat{\sigma}_\infty^2(\hat{\lambda}) = U/[n(2 - U_1)^4] \qquad [3.21]$$

where

$$U = (2 - U_1)(2 - U_2)(U_1 + U_2 + 4 - 2U_3)$$

$$- 2(2 - U_1)^2 \left(1 - n^{-1} \sum_{i}^{*} n_{im} \right) - 2(2 - U_2)^2 (1 - n_{m_r m_c}/n)$$

If all observations are concentrated in a single cell of the table, $U_1 = 2$ and equation 3.21 is undefined. Moreover, equation 3.21 is not uniquely defined if ties exist in the selection of row, column, or marginal maxima. Modifications in testing and estimation procedures recommended when $\hat{\lambda}_{A|B}$ is near 0 or 1 also apply to $\hat{\lambda}$. The estimate (equation 3.21) is not difficult to compute despite its formidable appearance. Calculations are illustrated in the following example.

Example 1. In an attempt to explain patterns in "witch-hunting" activities of various institutions by the extent to which societies express their corporate national interest (as measured by type of party system), Bergeson (1977) presents the data shown in Table 2. Can the number of political parties (B) be used to predict a country's institutional witch-hunting behavior (A), and vice versa?

Using the notation developed to write equation 3.21, we get

$$m_c = 1, \quad n_{mm_c} = 549, \quad n_{+m_c} = 2076$$

$$m_r = 1, \quad n_{m_r m} = 549, \quad n_{m_r+} = 815$$

$$\sum_i n_{im} = 2107, \quad \sum_j n_{mj} = 914$$

$$\sum_i^r n_{im_c} = 1983, \quad \sum_j^c n_{m_r j} = 761, \quad \text{and} \quad \sum_i^* n_{im} = 549.$$

Furthermore, $U_1 = (2076 + 815)/3077 = 0.93955$, $U_2 = (2107 + 914)/3077 = 0.98180$, and $U_3 = (1983 + 761 + 549 + 549)/3077 = 1.24862$.

For these data, equations 3.15, 3.16, and 3.17 have the values:

$$\hat{\lambda}_{A|B} = \frac{914 - 815}{3077 - 815} = \frac{99}{2262} = 0.0438$$

$$\hat{\lambda}_{B|A} = \frac{2107 - 2076}{3077 - 2076} = \frac{31}{1001} = 0.0310$$

$$\hat{\lambda} = \frac{99 + 31}{2262 + 1001} = \frac{130}{3263} = 0.0398$$

respectively. From equations 3.19, 3.20, and 3.21 we obtain the corresponding variance estimates: $\hat{\sigma}_\infty^2(\hat{\lambda}_{A|B}) = 0.3869 \times 10^{-4}$, $\hat{\sigma}_\infty^2(\hat{\lambda}_{B|A}) = 0.2099 \times 10^{-3}$, and $\hat{\sigma}_\infty^2(\hat{\lambda}) = 0.3478 \times 10^{-4}$.

Each estimator, when compared with its standard deviation, is significantly different from zero. The reduction in predictive error is small but statistically significant because of the large sample size. It is doubtful that the reduction is of practical significance, even granting that it is meaningful to make inferences about the "population" of witch hunts.

The chi-square statistic (equation 2.2) has the value $X^2 = 437.2$ for these data, so the two variables are clearly not independent. By way of comparison, the computed values of the measures based upon X^2 are $\hat{p} = 0.3527$, $\hat{p}^* = 0.4320$, $\hat{t} = 0.2025$, and $\hat{v} = 0.2665$. When compared with its standard deviation, each estimator turns out to be significantly different from zero. We reach the same conclusion in all cases: Association between the two variables is weak, but significant.

TABLE 2
Distribution of Witch-Hunting Activities by Institution
and Political Party System, 1950-1970

Institutional Areas (A)	Type of Political Party System (B)			
	One-Party	Two-Party	Multiparty	Totals
Government	549	212	54	815
Military	93	124	54	271
Education	233	78	33	344
Economy	119	42	13	174
Intellectuals	225	41	46	312
Religion	455	12	7	474
Foreigners	402	132	153	687
Totals	2076	641	360	3077

SOURCE: Bergeson (1977).

The most extensive discussion of the measures $\lambda_{A|B}$, $\lambda_{B|A}$, and λ, origi-
nally proposed by Guttman (1941), is contained in the papers of Goodman
and Kruskal (1954, 1963), in which the measures are defined, their asymptotic distributions are derived, numerical examples are given, and various
related measures are discussed. These measures are also discussed by Hays
(1963), Reynolds (1977a), and Bishop et al. (1975). Each treatment includes
numerical examples.

THE GOODMAN-KRUSKAL τ

The Goodman-Kruskal τ is derived like λ, except that a different
classification rule is used. Suppose the (marginal) distribution of the row
variable A is known, and, with only that information, the task is to estimate
the A category of a randomly selected member of the population. In this
case, classification must be accomplished so as to reproduce the marginal
distribution of A. Thus the individual is assigned to category 1 with probability p_{1+}, to category 2 with probability p_{2+}, and so on. The individual is
classified into class i with probability p_{i+}. That assignment is correct with
probability p_{i+}; consequently, the individual is correctly classified *into
class i* with probability p_{i+}^2. If this argument is applied to all I categories, it
turns out that the individual is correctly classified with probability

$$p_{1+}^2 + p_{2+}^2 + \ldots + p_{I+}^2 = \sum_{i=1}^{I} p_{i+}^2$$

and misclassified with probability

$$1 - \sum_{i=1}^{I} p_{i+}^2 \qquad [3.22]$$

Now suppose we know that the individual falls into class j of a second (column) variable B. By applying the classification rule to the probabilities in column j, we must assign the individual (conditionally) to row i with probability p_{ij}/p_{+j}. (The probability p_{ij}/p_{+j} is the conditional probability that A = i, given B = j.) In this case, the *conditional* probability of misclassification turns out to be

$$1 - \sum_{i=1}^{I} (p_{ij}/p_{+j})^2$$

while the *unconditional* probability of misclassification is

$$\sum_{j=1}^{J} P(\text{Error} \mid B = j) \, P(B = j) = \sum_{j=1}^{J} \left[1 - \sum_{i=1}^{I} (p_{ij}/p_{+j})^2 \right] p_{+j}$$

$$= 1 - \sum_{j=1}^{J} \sum_{i=1}^{I} (p_{ij}^2/p_{+j}) \qquad [3.23]$$

The relative decrease in the probability of an incorrect prediction is, from equations 3.22 and 3.23:

$$\tau_{A|B} = \frac{\left(1 - \sum_{i=1}^{I} p_{i+}^2\right) - \left(1 - \sum_{j=1}^{J} \sum_{i=1}^{I} (p_{ij}^2/p_{+j})\right)}{1 - \sum_{i=1}^{I} p_{i+}^2}$$

$$= \frac{\sum_{j=1}^{J} \sum_{i=1}^{I} p_{ij}^2/p_{+j} - \sum_{i=1}^{I} p_{i+}^2}{1 - \sum_{i=1}^{I} p_{i+}^2} \qquad [3.24]$$

Unless all nonzero probabilities of the table are in a single row, $\tau_{A|B}$ is well defined. The measure ranges from 0 to 1, and can assume both extreme values. In a column j that contains exactly one nonzero entry, there is some row i for which $p_{ij} = p_{+j}$. If each column contains exactly one nonzero entry, equation 3.23 equals 0 and $\tau_{A|B} = 1$. Thus knowledge of an individual's B category permits prediction of his or her A category with certainty. If A and B are independent, on the other hand, then $p_{ij} = p_{i+} \, p_{+j}$ for each i, j, and $\tau_{A|B} = 0$. Here, too, it can happen that one variable is of no help in predicting another, even though the variables are not independent.

By interchanging the roles of A and B, we obtain the measure

$$\tau_{B|A} = \frac{\sum\limits_{i=1}^{I} \sum\limits_{j=1}^{J} p_{ij}^2/p_{i+} - \sum\limits_{j=1}^{J} p_{+j}^2}{1 - \sum\limits_{j=1}^{J} p_{+j}^2} \qquad [3.25]$$

which is the relative reduction in the error of predicting the B category of an individual resulting from knowledge of his or her A classification.

If no natural asymmetry exists between the variables under consideration, the measure

$$\tau = \frac{\tau_{A|B}\left(1 - \sum\limits_{i=1}^{I} p_{i+}^2\right) + \tau_{B|A}\left(1 - \sum\limits_{j=1}^{J} p_{+j}^2\right)}{\left(1 - \sum\limits_{i=1}^{I} p_{i+}^2\right) + \left(1 - \sum\limits_{j=1}^{J} p_{+j}^2\right)}$$

$$= \frac{\sum\limits_{i=1}^{I} \sum\limits_{j=1}^{J} p_{ij}^2/p_{i+} + \sum\limits_{i=1}^{I} \sum\limits_{j=1}^{J} p_{ij}^2/p_{+j} - \sum\limits_{i=1}^{I} p_{i+}^2 - \sum\limits_{j=1}^{J} p_{+j}^2}{2 - \sum\limits_{i=1}^{I} p_{i+}^2 - \sum\limits_{j=1}^{J} p_{+j}^2} \qquad [3.26]$$

has been proposed. Suppose that a member of the population is selected at random from the population and that half the time the task is to predict his or her A category and half the time to predict his or her A category and half the time to predict his or her B category. Then τ can be interpreted as the reduction in probability of prediction error resulting from knowledge of the individual's classification on the second variable relative to the probability of error in absence of that information.

The measure τ is well defined if at least two cells, not both in the same row or column of the table, contain nonzero probabilities. The value of τ lies between the values of $\tau_{A|B}$ and $\tau_{B|A}$; consequently $0 \leqslant \tau \leqslant 1$. If the table has exactly one nonzero probability in each row and column, then $\tau = 1$, while $\tau = 0$ when A and B are independent.

Under the multinomial sampling model, $\tau_{A|B}$, $\tau_{B|A}$, and τ have maximum likelihood estimators

$$\hat{\tau}_{A|B} = \frac{n \sum\limits_{i=1}^{I} \sum\limits_{j=1}^{J} (n_{ij}^2/n_{+j}) - \sum\limits_{i=1}^{I} n_{i+}^2}{n^2 - \sum\limits_{i=1}^{I} n_{i+}^2} \qquad [3.27]$$

$$\hat{\tau}_{B|A} = \frac{n \sum_{j=1}^{J} \sum_{i=1}^{I} (n_{ij}^2/n_{i+}) - \sum_{j=1}^{J} n_{+j}^2}{n^2 - \sum_{j=1}^{J} n_{+j}^2} \qquad [3.28]$$

and

$$\hat{\tau} = \frac{n \left[\sum_{i=1}^{I} \sum_{j=1}^{J} (n_{ij}^2/n_{+j}) + \sum_{j=1}^{J} \sum_{i=1}^{I} (n_{ij}^2/n_{i+}) \right] - \sum_{j=1}^{J} n_{+j}^2 - \sum_{i=1}^{I} n_{i+}^2}{2n^2 - \sum_{j=1}^{J} n_{+j}^2 - \sum_{i=1}^{I} n_{i+}^2} \qquad [3.29]$$

respectively. If "probability" is replaced by "observed frequency," statements about the minimum, maximum, and range of equations 3.24, 2.25, and 3.26 apply also to equations 3.27, 2.28, and 3.29, respectively. If any one of the measures is either 0 or 1, the corresponding estimator has the same value.

Using Gini's definition of total variation in a sample from a categorical variable, Light and Margolin (1971) use methods analogous to those for partitioning a sum of squares in analysis of variance to derive a measure R^2 for contingency tables. It turns out (Margolin and Light, 1974) that R^2 is equivalent to the Goodman-Kruskal τ.

If the columns of the table represent the levels of some control variable B, Gini (1912) defines the total sum of squares (TSS) in the response variable A as

$$TSS = \frac{n}{2} - \frac{1}{2n} \sum_{i=1}^{I} n_{i+}^2 \qquad [3.30]$$

Further, equation 3.30 can be partitioned into a within-group sum of squares (WSS) and a between-group sum of squares (BSS):

$$WSS = \frac{n}{2} - \frac{1}{2} \sum_{j=1}^{J} \sum_{i=1}^{I} (n_{ij}^2/n_{+j})$$

$$BSS = TSS - WSS = \frac{1}{2} \sum_{i=1}^{I} \sum_{j=1}^{J} (n_{ij} - n_{i+}n_{+j}/n)^2 n_{+j}$$

Some algebra shows that the ratio of BSS and WSS is

$$\hat{R}^2_{A|B} = \frac{BSS}{TSS} = \frac{n \sum_{i=1}^{I} \sum_{j=1}^{J} (n_{ij} - n_{i+}n_{+j}/n)^2/n_{+j}}{n^2 - \sum_{i=1}^{I} n_{i+}^2} = \hat{\tau}_{A|B} \qquad [3.31]$$

The form of $\tau_{A\,B}$ suggested by equation 3.31 is one that resembles the parameter ϕ^2. In fact, $\phi^2 = (I - 1)\tau$ if $p_{i+} = 1/I$ for each i. Likewise, $X^2 = n(I - 1)\hat{\tau}_{A|B}$ if $n_{i+} = n/I$ for each i.

The Margolin-Light derivation gives us another interpretation of the measure τ. Like the correlation coefficient, $\tau_{A|B}$ is the proportion of variability in A that is attributable to, or explained by, B. But unlike the correlation coefficient, $\tau_{A|B}$ is not symmetric in its treatment of the two variables.

The exact sampling distributions of equations 3.27, 3.28, and 3.29 are unknown, but all three estimators are approximately normal for large samples under the multinomial sampling model. The asymptotic mean of each estimator is the corresponding population parameter. Provided that $\tau_{A|B}$ is not 0 or 1 and that $p_{i+} < 1$ for all i, Goodman and Kruskal (1972) give the following estimator of the asymptotic variance of $\hat{\tau}_{A|B}$:

$$\hat{\sigma}^2_{\infty}(\hat{\tau}_{A|B}) = \frac{1}{n^2\delta^4} \sum_{i=1}^{I} \sum_{j=1}^{J} n_{ij}(\hat{\phi}_{ij} - \hat{\bar{\phi}})^2 \qquad [3.32]$$

in which

$$\hat{\nu} = 1 - \sum_{i=1}^{I} \sum_{j=1}^{J} \left(\frac{n_{ij}}{n}\right)^2 \bigg/ \left(\frac{n}{n_{+j}}\right) = \frac{1}{n}\left(n - \sum_{i=1}^{I} \sum_{j=1}^{J} n_{ij}^2/n_{+j}\right) \qquad [3.33]$$

$$\hat{\delta} = 1 - \sum_{i=1}^{I} \left(\frac{n_{i+}}{n}\right)^2 = \frac{1}{n^2}\left(n^2 - \sum_{i=1}^{I} n_{i+}^2\right) \qquad [3.34]$$

$$\hat{\bar{\phi}} = \hat{\delta}(\hat{\nu} + 1) - 2\hat{\nu}$$

and

$$\hat{\phi}_{ij} = -2\hat{\nu}\left(\frac{n_{i+}}{n}\right) + 2\hat{\delta}\left(\frac{n_{ij}}{n}\right)\left(\frac{n}{n_{+j}}\right) - \hat{\delta}\sum_{k=1}^{I}\left(\frac{n_{kj}}{n_{+j}}\right)^2$$

$$= -2\hat{\nu}\left(\frac{n_{i+}}{n}\right) + \hat{\delta}\left[\frac{2n_{ij}}{n_{+j}} - \sum_{k=1}^{I}\left(\frac{n_{kj}}{n_{+j}}\right)^2\right] \qquad [3.35]$$

An estimator of the asymptotic variance of $\hat{\tau}_{B|A}$ can be obtained from equations 3.32, 3.33, 3.34, and 3.35 by interchanging the roles of i and j. The asymptotic variance of $\hat{\tau}$ is unpublished.

The asymptotic distribution of $\hat{\tau}_{A|B}$ can be used to perform significance tests and set up confidence intervals, provided that $\hat{\tau}_{A|B}$ is not equal to zero or one. The distributional properties given by Goodman and Kruskal cannot be used to test the hypothesis of independence since they do not hold for $\tau = 0$. However, $\hat{R}^2_{A|B} = \hat{\tau}_{A|B}$ when $\tau = 0$. Light and Margolin (1971) have shown that in this case the statistic

$$U^2_{A|B} = (n - 1)(I - 1)\hat{R}^2_{A|B} = (n - 1)(I - 1)\hat{\tau}_{A|B} \qquad [3.36]$$

is approximately distributed as a chi-square variable with $(I - 1)(J - 1)$ degrees of freedom. By symmetry,

$$U^2_{B|A} = (n - 1)(J - 1)\hat{R}^2_{B|A} = (n - 1)(J - 1)\hat{\tau}_{B|A} \qquad [3.37]$$

has the same asymptotic null distribution as $U^2_{A|B}$.

To continue the comparisons begun in the previous section, the values of $\hat{\tau}_{A|B}$, $\hat{\tau}_{B|A}$, and $\hat{\tau}$ are computed for the data of Example 1.

Example 1 (continued). Let

$$U_1 = \frac{1}{2076}(549^2 + 93^2 + \ldots + 455^2 + 402^2)$$

$$+ \frac{1}{641}(212^2 + 124^2 + \ldots + 12^2 + 132^2)$$

$$+ \frac{1}{360}(54^2 + 54^2 + \ldots + 7^2 + 153^2)$$

$$= 611.3839$$

$$U_2 = \frac{1}{815}(549^2 + 212^2 + 54^2) + \frac{1}{271}(93^2 + 124^2 + 54^2)$$

$$+ \ldots + \frac{1}{687}(402^2 + 132^2 + 153^2)$$

$$= 1705.3836$$

$$U_3 = 815^2 + 271^2 + \ldots + 474^2 + 687^2$$

$$= 1,680,267$$

$$U_4 = 2076^2 + 641^2 + 360^2$$

$$= 4,850,257$$

Then, from equations 3.27, 3.28, and 3.29

$$\hat{\tau}_{A|B} = \frac{nU_1 - U_3}{n^2 - U_3} = \frac{200,961.1829}{7,787,662} = 0.0258$$

$$\hat{\tau}_{B|A} = \frac{nU_2 - U_4}{n^2 - U_4} = \frac{397,208.4357}{4,617,672} = 0.0861$$

and

$$\hat{\tau} = \frac{200,961.1829 + 397,208.4357}{7,787,662 + 4,617,672} = 0.0482$$

The hypothesis $H_0^{(1)}$: $\tau_{A|B} = 0$ and $H_0^{(2)}$: $\tau_{B|A} = 0$ can be tested using equations 3.36 and 3.37. For these data, $U_{A|B}^2 = 3076 \times 6 \times (0.0258) = 476.2$ and $U_{B|A}^2 = 3076 \times 2 \times (0.0861) = 529.7$; both are significantly different from zero. The association between the two variables is statistically significant but of questionable practical significance because the improvement in predictability and the amount of explained variability are so slight.

The estimated asymptotic standard deviations of $\hat{\tau}_{A|B}$ and $\hat{\tau}_{B|A}$ can be computed from equation 3.32 and its symmetric counterpart: $\hat{\sigma}_\infty(\hat{\tau}_{A|B}) = (0.61386 \times 10^{-5})^{1/2} = 0.00248$ and $\hat{\sigma}_\infty(\hat{\tau}_{B|A}) = (0.48005 \times 10^{-4})^{1/2} = 0.00693$. These values can be used to construct confidence intervals for $\tau_{A|B}$ and $\tau_{B|A}$.

We cannot compute the variance of $\hat{\tau}$ directly, but the conservative method used here will often suffice. First, notice that

$$\sigma^2(aX_1 + bX_2) \leqslant [a\sigma(X_1) + b\sigma(X_2)]^2$$

for any two random variables (X_1, X_2) and any two constants (a, b). Now notice that

$$\hat{\tau} = a\hat{\tau}_{A|B} + (1 - a)\hat{\tau}_{B|A} \qquad [3.38]$$

where

$$a = \frac{n^2 - \sum\limits_{i=1}^{I} n_{i+}^2}{2n^2 - \sum\limits_{i=1}^{I} n_{i+}^2 - \sum\limits_{j=1}^{J} n_{+j}^2}$$

By setting $b = 1 - a$, $X_1 = \hat{\tau}_{A|B}$ and $X_2 = \hat{\tau}_{B|A}$ in equation 3.38, we see that

$$\hat{\sigma}_\infty^2(\hat{\tau}) \leqslant [0.62777 \ \hat{\sigma}_\infty(\hat{\tau}_{A|B}) + 0.37223 \ \hat{\sigma}_\infty(\hat{\tau}_{B|A})]^2$$

$$= (0.004134)^2 = 0.1709 \times 10^{-4}$$

Consequently, τ is also significantly different from zero.

The Goodman-Kruskal tau was first proposed by W. Allen Wallis. Goodman and Kruskal (1954, 1963, 1972) give asymptotic distributions under both the multinomial sampling model and the "product-multinomial" model (independent multinomial sampling at each level of one of the variables). Elementary discussions, with examples, are found in Blalock (1972), Reynolds (1977a, 1977b) and Bishop et al. (1975). Margolin and Light, in two joint papers (1974; Light and Margolin, 1971), demonstrate the equivalence of $\hat{R}_{A|B}^2$ and $\hat{\tau}_{A|B}$.

Measures of Agreement

As used so far, the term "association" is rather general. Two variables are said to be associated if they are not independent, or if one is useful in predicting the other. It is often of interest to measure *agreement*, which is a specific type of association. Suppose each of two judges (or raters) A and B independently classify items into one of I mutually exclusive categories, and we want a measure of agreement between the judges. In contingency table notation, n_{ij} is the number of objects assigned to category i by A and category j by B. The following simple example illustrates that a table may exhibit high association, but little or no agreement. Suppose ten items are classified by two judges as shown in the following table:

		B	
		1	2
A	1	0	5
	2	5	0

In terms of predictability, the ratings are perfectly associated, but the raters certainly are not in agreement!

How can agreement be measured? Surely, two judges agree on a given item if both assign it to the same category. The diagonal frequencies n_{11}, $n_{22}, \ldots, n_{II}$ are therefore of primary importance in measuring agreement. Three measures specifically constructed to measure agreement are discussed below.

COHEN'S κ AND WEIGHTED κ

Let p_{ij} denote the probability that an item is classified into category i by one judge and category j by another, where i and j range from 1 to I, inclusive. Then

$$\theta_1 = \sum_{i=1}^{I} p_{ii} \qquad [3.39]$$

represents the proportion of cases on which the judges agree. If the judges work independently, the proportion of times they agree purely by chance is

$$\theta_2 = \sum_{i=1}^{I} p_{i+} p_{+i} \qquad [3.40]$$

so $\theta_1 - \theta_2$ is a measure of agreement corrected for chance. To make this measure independent of the marginal totals, it is normalized by $1 - \theta_2$, the maximum possible value of $\theta_1 - \theta_2$ for the given sets of marginal totals $\{p_{i+}\}$ and $\{p_{+i}\}$. The resulting measure,

$$\kappa = \frac{\theta_1 - \theta_2}{1 - \theta_2} \qquad [3.41]$$

was proposed by Cohen (1960) as a measure of agreement, corrected for chance, between the classifications of a group of objects by two judges. Cohen's κ can also be interpreted as a measure of agreement between pairs of individuals, all of which are responding on the same scale to a given issue.

Values of κ can range from $-\theta_2/(1 - \theta_2)$ to 1 for a given set of marginal totals. If the judges are in complete agreement, $\theta_1 = 1$ and $\kappa = 1$, while $\kappa = -\theta_2/(1 - \theta_2)$ if the judges disagree completely. If the two classifications are independent so that $p_{i+} p_{+i} = p_{ii}$ for each i, $\theta_1 = \theta_2$ and $\kappa = 0$. It is possible to have $\kappa = 0$ even if the classifications are not independent. The measure in equation 3.41 is well defined if at least two cells of the table contain nonzero probabilities.

The maximum likelihood estimator of κ under the multinomial sampling model is

$$\hat{\kappa} = \frac{n \sum_{i=1}^{I} n_{ii} - \sum_{i=1}^{I} n_{i+} n_{+i}}{n^2 - \sum_{i=1}^{I} n_{i+} n_{+i}}$$

When p_{ij} is replaced by $\hat{p}_{ij} = n_{ij}/n$, statements about the range of κ apply also to $\hat{\kappa}$.

For n sufficiently large, $\hat{\kappa}$ is approximately a normal variable with mean κ. The approximate large sample variance of $\hat{\kappa}$ is

$$\sigma_\infty^2(\hat{\kappa}) = \frac{1}{n} \left\{ \frac{\theta_1(1-\theta_1)}{(1-\theta_2)^2} + \frac{2(1-\theta_1)(2\theta_1\theta_2 - \theta_3)}{(1-\theta_2)^3} \right.$$
$$\left. + \frac{(1-\theta_1)^2(\theta_4 - 4\theta_2^2)}{(1-\theta_2)^4} \right\} \qquad [3.42]$$

where θ_1 and θ_2 are defined by equations 3.39 and 3.40, respectively, and where

$$\theta_3 = \sum_{i=1}^{I} p_{ii}(p_{i+} + p_{+i}) \quad \text{and} \quad \theta_4 = \sum_{i=1}^{I} \sum_{j=1}^{J} p_{ij}(p_{j+} + p_{+i})^2$$

Under the hypothesis of independence, equation 3.42 reduces to

$$\sigma_\infty^2(\hat{\kappa}) = \frac{1}{n(1-\theta_2)^2} \left[\theta_2 + \theta_2^2 - \sum_{i=1}^{I} p_{i+} p_{+i}(p_{i+} + p_{+i}) \right] \qquad [3.43]$$

Estimators of equations 3.42 and 3.43 are obtained as usual by substituting $\hat{p}_{ij} = n_{ij}/n$ for p_{ij}. The estimator obtained from equation 3.43 can be used to test the hypothesis $\kappa = 0$, while equation 3.42 can be used to establish confidence intervals for κ.

The calculations of $\hat{\kappa}$ and its variance are illustrated in the next example.

Example 2. Suppose 100 married couples are selected, and each spouse is asked to classify his or her marriage as happy (H), unhappy (U), or about average (A). The (fictitious) results are summarized in Table 3.

From equations 3.39 and 3.40 we get $\hat{\theta}_1 = 0.73$, $\hat{\theta}_2 = 0.335$, $\hat{\theta}_3 = 0.4935$, and $\hat{\theta}_4 = 0.4755$. Thus,

$$\hat{\kappa} = \frac{0.73 - 0.335}{1 - 0.335} = 0.5940$$

and its estimated large sample variance is, from equation 3.42,

$$\hat{\sigma}_\infty^2(\hat{\kappa}) = 0.004475 \qquad\qquad [3.44]$$

Approximate confidence intervals can be based on equation 3.44. However, this value should be replaced by $\hat{\sigma}_\infty^2(\hat{\kappa}) = 0.01983$ when testing the hypothesis $\kappa = 0$. From either a significance test or a confidence interval, we conclude that husbands and wives are in significantly greater agreement about their marriages than would be expected by chance.

Several extensions of κ have been proposed. One of the more important comes from introducing weights that permit the assignment of "degrees of agreement" to various responses. It could be argued in Example 2 that there is more agreement between a husband and wife who respond (H, A) than between a couple whose response is (H, U). If such comparisons can somehow be quantified in a meaningful way, this information can be incorporated into the calculation of κ by assigning a weight w_{ij} to each response category (i, j). In defining the weighted version of κ, Cohen (1968) requires (without loss of generality) that $0 \leqslant w_{ij} \leqslant 1$ and assumes that weights are interpretable as ratios; e.g., the weight 0.75 represents three times the agreement of the weight 0.25. With

$$\theta_1^* = \sum_{i=1}^{I} \sum_{j=1}^{J} w_{ij} P_{ij}$$

and

$$\theta_2^* = \sum_{i=1}^{I} \sum_{j=1}^{J} w_{ij} P_{i+} P_{+j}$$

the weighted version of kappa is defined by

$$\kappa_w = \frac{\theta_1^* - \theta_2^*}{1 - \theta_2^*}$$

Values of κ_w can range from $-\theta_2^*/(1 - \theta_2^*)$ to 1 for a given set of marginal totals. If the two ratings are in complete agreement, $\kappa_w = 1$, while $\kappa_w = 0$ if the two classifications are independent. The measure κ_w is well defined if at least two cells of the table contain nonzero probabilities.

The maximum likelihood estimator of κ_w under the multinomial sampling model is

$$\hat{\kappa}_w = \frac{n \sum\limits_{i=1}^{I} \sum\limits_{j=1}^{J} w_{ij} n_{ij} - \sum\limits_{i=1}^{I} \sum\limits_{j=1}^{J} w_{ij} n_{i+} n_{+j}}{n^2 - \sum\limits_{i=1}^{I} \sum\limits_{j=1}^{J} w_{ij} n_{i+} n_{+j}}$$

Statements about the range of κ_w apply to $\hat{\kappa}_w$ as well. For large samples, $\hat{\kappa}_w$ is approximately a normal variable with expected value κ_w and variance

$$\sigma_\infty^2(\hat{\kappa}_w) = \frac{1}{n(1-\theta_2^*)^4} \left\{ \sum\limits_{i=1}^{I} \sum\limits_{j=1}^{J} p_{ij} [w_{ij}(1-\theta_2^*) \right.$$

$$\left. - (\bar{w}_{i+} + \bar{w}_{+j})(1-\theta_1^*)]^2 - (\theta_1^*\theta_2^* - 2\theta_2^* + \theta_1^*)^2 \right\} \quad [3.45]$$

where

$$\bar{w}_{i+} = \sum\limits_{j=1}^{J} w_{ij} p_{+j}$$

and

$$\bar{w}_{+j} = \sum\limits_{i=1}^{I} w_{ij} p_{i+}$$

If the two ratings are independent so that $\theta_1^* = \theta_2^*$ and $p_{ij} = p_{i+} p_{ij}$, equation 3.45 simplifies to

$$\sigma_\infty^2(\hat{\kappa}_w) = \frac{1}{n(1-\theta_2^*)^2} \left\{ \sum\limits_{i=1}^{I} \sum\limits_{j=1}^{J} p_{i+} p_{+j} [w_{ij} \right.$$

$$\left. - (\bar{w}_{i+} + \bar{w}_{+j})]^2 - \theta_2^{*2} \right\} \quad [3.46]$$

An estimate obtained from equation 3.46 can be used to test the hypothesis $\kappa_w = 0$, but equation 3.45 should be used in testing other hypotheses or for constructing confidence intervals.

Note that κ is a special case of κ_w. If

$$w_{ij} = \begin{cases} 1, i = j \\ 0, i \neq j \end{cases} \quad [3.47]$$

then $\kappa_w = \kappa$ and $\hat{\kappa}_w = \hat{\kappa}$. Furthermore, if equation 3.47 holds, $\bar{w}_{i+} = p_{+i}$ and $\bar{w}_{+j} = p_{j+}$, so equations 3.45 and 3.46 reduce to equations 3.42 and 3.43, respectively.

Example 2 (continued). We shall calculate $\hat{\kappa}_w$ for the data of Table 3 using the following weight matrix.

		Wife		
		H	A	U
Husband	H	1.0	0.5	0.0
	A	0.5	1.0	0.5
	U	0.0	0.5	1.0

Since $\hat{\theta}_1^* = 0.855$ and $\hat{\theta}_2^* = 0.570$,

$$\hat{\kappa}_w = \frac{0.855 - 0.570}{1 - 0.570} = 0.6628$$

Further, $\overline{w}_{1+}, \overline{w}_{2+}, \overline{w}_{3+}, \overline{w}_{+1}, \overline{w}_{+2}$, and $\overline{w}_{+3}$ have the values 0.575, 0.675, 0.425, 0.5, 0.7, and 0.7 respectively, so equation 3.45 yields

$$\hat{\sigma}_\infty^2(\hat{\kappa}_w) = 0.003449 \qquad [3.48]$$

This value (equation 3.48) can be used for making inferences about κ_w, except that the value $\hat{\sigma}_\infty^2(\hat{\kappa}) = 0.005829$ obtained from equation 3.46 should be used for testing the hypothesis $\kappa_w = 0$.

The measures κ and κ_w were proposed by Cohen in 1960 and 1968, respectively. The main properties of both estimators are contained in the paper by Fleiss, Cohen, and Everitt (1969), as well as in the more recent books of Bishop et al. (1975) and Reynolds (1977a). All references cited contain numerical examples. Fleiss (1971) and Light (1971) have generalized κ to measure agreement between more than two groups or judges.

TABLE 3
Self-Assessment of Marital Happiness by 100 Couples

		Wife			
		H(1)	A(2)	U(3)	n_{i+}
	H(1)	28	2	0	30
Husband	A(2)	10	25	5	40
	U(3)	2	8	20	30
	n_{+j}	40	35	25	100

THE COLEMAN-LIGHT MEASURE OF CONDITIONAL AGREEMENT

The Coleman-Light measure of conditional agreement is similar to κ, except that here probabilities are calculated conditionally with respect to a particular rating of one of the judges. Now let A_i (or B_i) denote the event that an item is assigned to category i by rater A (or B), and suppose that we are interested in agreement only for those items classified into a particular category i (a row of the table) by rater A. The conditional probability that B places the item in category i, given that A has placed it in category i, is

$$\theta_1^* = P(B_i|A_i) = \frac{P(A_i B_i)}{P(A_i)} = \frac{p_{ii}}{p_{i+}}$$

Likewise, assuming independence,

$$\theta_2^* = p_{i+}p_{+i}/p_{i+} = p_{+i}$$

The conditional agreement between the two raters for those items assigned to the ith category by the first is now defined as

$$\kappa_i = \frac{\theta_1^* - \theta_2^*}{1 - \theta_2^*} = \frac{\dfrac{p_{ii}}{p_{i+}} - p_{+i}}{1 - p_{+i}} = \frac{p_{ii} - p_{i+}p_{+i}}{p_{i+} - p_{i+}p_{+i}}$$

Values of κ_i can range from $-\theta_2^*/(1 - \theta_2^*)$ to 1 for given sets of marginals $\{p_{i+}\}$ and $\{p_{+i}\}$. In the case of perfect (conditional) agreement, $\kappa_i = 1$, while $\kappa_i = 0$ if the classifications are independent. By writing $\kappa_i = \nu_i/\delta_i$, it is easy to see that

$$\kappa = \sum_{i=1}^{I} \nu_i / \sum_{i=1}^{I} \delta_i$$

showing that κ is a weighted sum of the κ_is.

The maximum likelihood estimator of κ_i under the multinomial sampling model is

$$\hat{\kappa}_i = \frac{nn_{ii} - n_{i+}n_{+i}}{nn_{i+} - n_{i+}n_{+i}}$$

For large samples, $\hat{\kappa}_i$ is approximately a normal variable with mean κ_i and variance

$$\sigma_\infty^2(\hat{\kappa}_i) = \frac{1}{n} \frac{p_{i+} - p_{ii}}{p_{i+}^3 (1 - p_{+i})^3} [(p_{i+} - p_{ii})(p_{i+}p_{+i} - p_{ii})$$

$$+ p_{ii}(1 - p_{i+} - p_{+i} + p_{ii})] \qquad [3.49]$$

Under the hypothesis of independence, equation 3.49 becomes

$$\sigma_\infty^2(\hat{\kappa}_i) = \frac{1}{n} \frac{p_{+i}(1 - p_{i+})}{p_{i+}(1 - p_{+i})} \qquad [3.50]$$

Both equation 3.49 and equation 3.50 can be estimated by substituting observed proportions for cell probabilities. The latter should be used for testing $\kappa_i = 0$, but equation 3.49 should be used for all other inferences.

Example 2 (continued). Calculating the measure of agreement between husband and wife for each possible response of the husband from the data in Table 3, we get

$$\hat{\kappa}_1 = \frac{100 \times 28 - 30 \times 40}{100 \times 30 - 30 \times 40} = \frac{1600}{1800} = 0.8889$$

$$\hat{\kappa}_2 = \frac{100 \times 25 - 40 \times 35}{100 \times 40 - 40 \times 35} = \frac{1100}{2600} = 0.4231$$

$$\hat{\kappa}_3 = \frac{100 \times 20 - 30 \times 25}{100 \times 30 - 30 \times 25} = \frac{1250}{2250} = 0.5556$$

From equation 3.49 we obtain $\hat{\sigma}_\infty^2(\hat{\kappa}_1) = 0.0054595$. Likewise, $\hat{\sigma}_\infty^2(\hat{\kappa}_2) = 0.0092598$ and $\hat{\sigma}_\infty^2(\hat{\kappa}_3) = 0.010316$. For testing $H_0: \kappa_1 = 0$, the variance estimates obtained from equation 3.50 are $\hat{\sigma}_\infty^2(\hat{\kappa}_1) = 0.01556$, $\hat{\sigma}_\infty^2(\hat{\kappa}_2) = 0.008077$, and $\hat{\sigma}_\infty^2(\hat{\kappa}_3) = 0.007778$, respectively. All three measures are significantly different from zero, but it appears there is somewhat more agreement between couples in which the husband considers his marriage happy than in the other two cases. Finally, note that

$$\frac{1600 + 1100 + 1250}{1800 + 2600 + 2250} = \frac{3950}{6650} = 0.5940$$

which equals the earlier estimate of κ.

The measure κ_1 was first proposed by Coleman (1966) and has been studied in detail by Light (1969, 1971). All the results presented here, with another example, are found in Bishop et al. (1975).

Special Measures for 2×2 Contingency Tables

Fourfold tables provide a relatively simple context in which to study measures of association. Three constraints are required to ensure that cell probabilities add correctly, so a single probability placed in any cell of the table fixes the probabilities in the other three cells. In other words, there is only "one degree of freedom for association" in a fourfold table. Consequently, nearly all measures reduce to functions of either the cross-product (odds) ratio or the mean square contingency. Further, distinctions between symmetric and asymmetic measures disappear, as do distinctions between measures for ordinal and nominal data.

MEASURES BASED ON THE CROSS-PRODUCT RATIO

The cross-product ratio, or odds ratio, plays an important role in the construction of log-linear models. The cross-product ratio is defined by

$$\alpha = \frac{p_{11}p_{22}}{p_{12}p_{21}} = \frac{p_{11}/p_{12}}{p_{21}/p_{22}} = \frac{p_{11}/p_{21}}{p_{12}/p_{22}} \qquad [3.51]$$

The origin of the term "cross-product ratio" is evident from the first expression for α in equation 3.51, while the latter two expressions are the source of the term "odds ratio." Actually the "log odds ratio"

$$\alpha^* = \log \alpha$$

is often used instead of α because it has several nice mathematical properties. Because $\log \alpha^{-1} = -\log \alpha$, equal but opposite associations yield values of α^* with the same magnitude but opposite sign. The log odds ratio α^* is a symmetric measure that varies from $-\infty$ to ∞ and has the value $\log 1 = 0$ in the case of independence. The log odds ratio, like α, is unchanged if the rows of columns of the table are rescaled. The insensitivity of the odds ratio to marginal distribution means that comparisons can be made among tables obtained by sampling different populations (i.e., tables with different marginal distributions).

For present purposes, however, it is α which is of greatest interest. The maximum likelihood estimator of equation 3.51 under both the multinomial and product binomial[6] sampling models is

$$\hat{\alpha} = (n_{11}n_{22})/(n_{12}n_{21})$$

The estimator $\hat{\alpha}$ is approximately normally distributed for large samples under both the multinomial and product binomial models. Its asymptotic mean is α, and its approximate large sample variance is

$$\sigma_{\infty}^2(\hat{\alpha}) = \frac{\alpha^2}{n} \left(\frac{1}{p_{11}} + \frac{1}{p_{12}} + \frac{1}{p_{21}} + \frac{1}{p_{22}} \right) \tag{3.52}$$

Provided all cell counts are positive, an estimate of equation 3.52 obtained by replacing p_{ij} with $\hat{p}_{ij} = n_{ij}/n$: Thus

$$\hat{\sigma}_{\infty}^2(\hat{\alpha}) = \hat{\alpha}^2 \left(\frac{1}{n_{11}} + \frac{1}{n_{12}} + \frac{1}{n_{21}} + \frac{1}{n_{22}} \right) \tag{3.53}$$

If any observed frequency is zero, then formula 3.53 must be modified. One very simple modification is to add 0.5 to each cell count when any observed frequency is zero.

Two measures proposed by Yule are both functions of the cross-product ratio. Yule's (1900) "measure of association" is defined as

$$Q = \frac{p_{11}p_{22} - p_{12}p_{21}}{p_{11}p_{22} + p_{12}p_{21}} = \frac{\alpha - 1}{\alpha + 1} \tag{3.54}$$

and his "measure of colligation" (1912) is defined as

$$Y = \frac{\sqrt{p_{11}p_{22}} - \sqrt{p_{12}p_{21}}}{\sqrt{p_{11}p_{22}} + \sqrt{p_{12}p_{21}}} = \frac{\sqrt{\alpha} - 1}{\sqrt{\alpha} + 1} \tag{3.55}$$

Note that $Q = 2Y/(1 + Y^2)$. By replacing α with $\hat{\alpha}$ in equations 3.54 and 3.55 we obtain the estimators

$$\hat{Q} = \frac{\hat{\alpha} - 1}{\hat{\alpha} + 1} \tag{3.56}$$

and

$$\hat{Y} = \frac{\sqrt{\hat{\alpha}} - 1}{\sqrt{\hat{\alpha}} + 1} \tag{3.57}$$

respectively. Both Q and Y are maximum likelihood estimators under both the multinomial and product binomial models.

Both Y and Q are symmetric measures, both are unchanged by scale changes applied to rows or columns of the table, and both can assume all values between −1 and 1, inclusive. Both measures equal 1 when $\alpha = \infty$ (i.e., $p_{12}p_{21} = 0$), equal −1 if $\alpha = 0$ ($p_{11}p_{22} = 0$), and are 0 if $\alpha = 1$ (the case of independence). For other values of α, $|Y| < |Q|$, but the measures are consistent in the sense that $Q_1 > Q_2$ for a pair of tables whenever $Y_1 > Y_2$. The estimators $\hat{Q}$ and $\hat{Y}$ possess all the properties of Q and Y, respectively. Moreover, for large samples $\hat{Q}$ and $\hat{Y}$ are distributed approximately as normal variables with means Q and Y, respectively, and large-sample variables.

$$\sigma_\infty^2(\hat{Q}) = \frac{(1 - Q^2)^2}{4n} \left(\frac{1}{p_{11}} + \frac{1}{p_{12}} + \frac{1}{p_{21}} + \frac{1}{p_{22}} \right)$$

and

$$\sigma_\infty^2(\hat{Y}) = \frac{(1 - Y^2)^2}{16n} \left(\frac{1}{p_{11}} + \frac{1}{p_{12}} + \frac{1}{p_{21}} + \frac{1}{p_{22}} \right)$$

The corresponding estimators are

$$\hat{\sigma}_\infty^2(\hat{Q}) = \frac{(1 - \hat{Q}^2)^2}{4} \left(\frac{1}{n_{11}} + \frac{1}{n_{12}} + \frac{1}{n_{21}} + \frac{1}{n_{22}} \right) \qquad [3.58]$$

and

$$\hat{\sigma}_\infty^2(\hat{Y}) = \frac{(1 - \hat{Y}^2)^2}{16} \left(\frac{1}{n_{11}} + \frac{1}{n_{12}} + \frac{1}{n_{21}} + \frac{1}{n_{22}} \right) \qquad [3.59]$$

As with the variance of α, equations 3.58 and 3.59 cannot be used without modification if any cell frequency is zero.

What about meaningful interpretations of Yule's measures? Consider Q first. Denote the classifications with respect to the (dichotomous) variables A and B of two individuals selected at random from the population by (a_1, b_1) and (a_2, b_2). Three possibilities exist: the pairs are *concordant* if $(a_2 - a_1)(b_2 - b_1) > 0$, *discordant* if $(a_2 - a_1)(b_2 - b_1) > 0$, or *tied* if $a_1 = a_2$ or $b_1 = b_2$ (see the section on Kendall's τ in Chapter 4). These events have probabilities $2p_{11}p_{22}$, $2p_{12}p_{21}$, and $1 - 2(p_{11}p_{22} + p_{12}p_{21})$, respectively. Since $2(p_{11}p_{22} + p_{12}p_{21})$ is the probability that the pairs are not tied and

$$Q = \frac{p_{11}p_{22}}{p_{11}p_{22} + p_{12}p_{21}} - \frac{p_{12}p_{21}}{p_{11}p_{22} + p_{12}p_{21}}$$

Q is the difference between the conditional probability that the A and B scores are concordant (have like order) and the conditional probability that

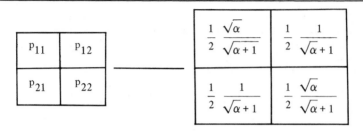

Figure 1: Construction of a Standardized Table

the scores are discordant (have unlike order), the condition in both cases being that scores are not tied.

For 2×2 tables, Yule's Q is identical to the Goodman-Kruskal γ (see the section on Measures Related to Kendall's τ_b in Chapter 5). The interpretation of Q given here is identical to that given for γ in Chapter 5.

The simplest interpretation of Yule's Y is given in terms of standardized tables. A standardized table results from adjusting the probabilities of a 2×2 table so that both row and column marginal totals become $(1/2, 1/2)$, while the cross-product ratio remains unchanged. The construction of a standardized table is shown in Figure 1. Let

$$p_{11}^* = p_{22}^* = \frac{1}{2} \frac{\sqrt{\alpha}}{\sqrt{\alpha} + 1}$$

and

$$p_{12}^* = p_{21}^* = \frac{1}{2} \frac{1}{\sqrt{\alpha} + 1}$$

Yule argues that standardization has removed all information about marginals, so a "reasonable measure of association" is the difference between the probabilities in the diagonal and off-diagonal cells. This difference is simply

$$(p_{11}^* + p_{22}^*) - (p_{12}^* + p_{21}^*) = \frac{\sqrt{\alpha} - 1}{\sqrt{\alpha} + 1} = Y$$

Finally, Y is a measure of proportional reduction in predictive error for standardized 2×2 tables, since then all versions of both the Goodman-Kruskal τ and the Goodman-Kruskal λ are equal to $|Y|$.

The measures Q and Y were originally studied by Yule (1900, 1912). Thorough discussions of measures of association based upon the odds ratio are given by Bishop et al. (1975) and Reynolds (1977a). Both contain numerical examples.

MEASURES BASED ON THE CORRELATION COEFFICIENT

The Pearson product-moment correlation coefficient has been so widely used for so long with continuous data that it is only natural to find modifications suitable for discrete data. For a 2×2 table in which the two levels of both row and column variables A and B are coded 0 and 1, Pearson's product-moment correlation coefficient (see equation 4.1 in Chapter 4) can be written as

$$\rho = \frac{p_{22} - p_{2+}p_{+2}}{(p_{1+}p_{2+}p_{+1}p_{+2})^{1/2}} = \frac{p_{11}p_{22} - p_{12}p_{21}}{(p_{1+}p_{2+}p_{+1}p_{+2})^{1/2}} \qquad [3.60]$$

We can see from equations 3.60 and 3.1 that $\rho^2 = \phi^2$; hence, measures based on the correlation coefficient are functions of Pearson's coefficient of mean square contingency and vice versa.

Since $\rho^2 = \phi^2$, measures based on one of them have the properties inherited from both. In particular, ρ is symmetric and remains unchanged if the rows or columns are scored by any positive linear transformation. If rows or columns, but not both, are interchanged, ρ changes sign; ρ is unchanged if both rows and columns are interchanged. Sinc ρ is a correlation coefficient, we know that $-1 \leqslant \rho \leqslant 1$. If A and B are independent, then $\rho = 0$. Moreover, $\rho = 1$ if $p_{12} = p_{21} = 0$, and conversely. Likewise, $\rho = -1$ if $p_{11} = p_{22} = 0$, and conversely.

The sign of ρ clearly depends on the labels assigned to the categories of A and B. This behavior is undesirable in a measure for nominal data because category labels are purely arbitrary. The use of ρ with fourfold (nominal) tables is an exception because it is easy to determine which categories are positively correlated regardless of the sign of ρ or how the categories are labeled.

Unlike the odds ratio, ρ is not independent of the marginal values of the table. For a standardized table, where the effect of marginal total has been removed, $\rho = Y$. For nonstandardized tables, $\rho = Y$ only if $\rho = 0, 1,$ or -1; otherwise, $|\rho| < |Y|$. For tables with a given cross-product ratio, the difference between ρ and Y tends to increase as the disparity between marginal totals increases.

For interpretive purposes, ρ is best viewed as a correlation coefficient (see the section on Pearson's Product-Moment Correlation in Chapter 4). As such, ρ^2 is the proportion of variability in one of the variables explained by knowledge of the other, and is a measure of the degree of colinearity between the two variables A and B.

The maximum likelihood estimator of ρ under the multinomial sampling model is

$$R = \frac{n_{11} n_{22} - n_{12} n_{21}}{(n_{1+} n_{2+} n_{+1} n_{+2})^{1/2}}$$

For large samples, R is approximately distributed as a normal variable with mean ρ and variance

$$\sigma_\infty^2(R) = \frac{1}{n} \left\{ (1 - \rho^2) + \left(1 + \frac{1}{2} \rho^2 \right) \frac{(p_{1+} - p_{2+})(p_{+1} - p_{+2})}{(p_{1+} p_{2+} p_{+1} p_{+2})^{1/2}} \right.$$
$$\left. - \frac{3}{4} \rho^2 \left[\frac{(p_{1+} - p_{2+})^2}{p_{1+} p_{2+}} + \frac{(p_{+1} - p_{+2})^2}{p_{+1} p_{+2}} \right] \right\} \qquad [3.61]$$

Equation 3.61 reduces to $\sigma_\infty^2(R) = 1/n$ under the hypothesis of independence, and to $\sigma_\infty^2(R) = (1 - \rho^2)/n$ for a standardized table. To estimate $\sigma_\infty^2(R)$, we substitute $\hat{p}_{ij} = n_{ij}/n$ for p_{ij} and the observed value of R for ρ in the appropriate formula.

Several equalities among various measures have already been mentioned. For any 2×2 table, Yule's Q is equal to the Goodman-Kruskal γ. Further, $\rho = Y$ for any standardized table, and all versions of the Goodman-Kruskal τ and Goodman-Kruskal λ equal $|Y|$. Also, ρ^2, ϕ^2, τ_b^2, $\tau_{A|B}^2$, $\tau_{B|A}^2$, and τ^2 are all equal for any 2×2 table.[7] Thus, of all the measures considered, only Q and ρ are distinct for fourfold tables.

The choice between Q and ρ is dictated by two considerations: (1) whether we want a measure sensitive to marginal totals, and (2) whether we want one that has the value ± 1 when only one cell of the table is zero.[8] Yule's Q is insensitive to marginal totals, while ρ is not. On the other hand, $Q = \pm 1$ when only one cell of the table is zero, but unequal marginal totals can constrain the upper limit for $|\rho|$ to be less than one.

Bishop et al. (1975) and Reynolds (1977a) discuss measures based on the correlation coefficient. Both contain numerical examples.

4. MEASURES OF CORRELATION FOR CONTINUOUS (INTERVAL) DATA

Pearson's product-moment correlation coefficient and Spearman's rank correlation coefficient are among the oldest measures of association. The product-moment correlation coefficient is still one of the most widely used. Nearly all the measures for ordinal data can be traced to Kendall's coefficient of concordance. All three measures are discussed in this chapter.

We will suppose throughout this chapter that $(X_1, Y_1), \ldots, (X_n, Y_n)$ is a random sample of size n from a continuous bivariate population (X, Y). We will also suppose that X and Y have means μ_X and μ_Y and variances σ_X^2 and σ_Y^2, respectively.

Theoretically, we need not worry about ties, because the probability is zero that two observations are tied on either X or Y, or both. Ties do occur in practice, however, and estimators that take them into account are quite naturally used for ordinal data.

Pearson's Product-Moment Correlation Coefficient

Since it was fashioned into a statistical tool by Galton, Edgeworth, and K. Pearson in the late nineteenth century, no measure of association has enjoyed such widespread use (and misuse) as the product-moment correlation coefficient. The product-moment correlation coefficient bears Pearson's name because of his famous 1896 paper dealing with its properties.

Let (X, Y) be a continuous bivariate population. Then the product-moment correlation coefficient is defined by

$$\rho = \frac{\text{Cov}(X, Y)}{\sigma_X \sigma_Y} = \frac{\sigma(X, Y)}{\sigma_X \sigma_Y} \qquad [4.1]$$

where σ_X and σ_Y are the standard deviations of X and Y, and $\sigma(X, Y)$ is the covariance between the two variables.[9]

Properties of equation 4.1 are closely related to the problem of linear prediction. The *linear prediction problem* is that of finding the best linear function of X to predict Y in the sense of minimizing the mean squared predictive error. That is, among all linear functions $h(X) = \alpha + \beta X$, we want the one which minimizes $E(Y - h(X))^2$. The best linear predictor of Y in terms of X is known to be

$$h^*(X) = \mu_Y + \frac{\sigma(X, Y)}{\sigma_X^2} (X - \mu_X) = \mu_Y + \frac{\rho \sigma_Y}{\sigma_X} (X - \mu_X)$$

$$= \alpha_1^* + \beta_1^* X \qquad [4.2]$$

where $\beta_1^* = \rho \sigma_Y / \sigma_X$ and $\alpha_1^* = \mu_Y - \beta_1 \mu_X$. The corresponding mean squared predictive error is

$$\text{MSPE}^* = \sigma_Y^2 (1 - \rho^2) \tag{4.3}$$

Note also that

$$V(h^*(X)) = V(\alpha_1^* + \beta_1^* X) = \sigma_Y^2 \rho^2 \tag{4.4}$$

The function h* is called the *linear regression of Y on X*.

Formulas 4.3 and 4.4 provide us with interpretations of ρ^2. From equation 4.3, we see that $1 - \rho^2$ is the proportion of variability in Y which is "free from X" or "unexplained by X." In other words, ρ^2 is the portion of the variance of Y that can be attributed to its linear regression on X, or that can be "explained" by its regression on X. If $\rho^2 = 1$, then all of σ_Y^2 is explained. In this case, all observations fall on the line

$$Y = \mu_Y + \rho \; \frac{\sigma_Y}{\sigma_X} \; (X - \mu_x)$$

If $\rho^2 = 0$, then MSPE* $= \rho_Y^2$, so no variability in Y is explained by its regression on X. It is important to remember that ρ is a measure of *linear* correlation. Formula 4.4 says that ρ^2 is the "variance of the 'best' estimate of Y based on X, relative to the variance of Y" (Kruskal, 1958: 817).

The roles of X and Y can be interchanged in the above discussion. If so, we obtain

$$g^*(Y) = \mu_X + \frac{\rho \sigma_X}{\sigma_Y} \; (Y - \mu_Y) = \alpha_2^* + \beta_2^* + \beta_2^* Y \tag{4.5}$$

as the *linear regression of X on Y*. In equation 4.5, we see that $\beta_2^* = \rho \sigma_X / \sigma_Y$. It follows from equations 4.2 and 4.5 that

$$\beta_1^* \beta_2^* = \frac{\rho \sigma_Y}{\sigma_X} \; \frac{\rho \sigma_X}{\sigma_Y} = \rho^2$$

The estimates obtained by minimizing

$$Q = \sum_{i=1}^{n} (Y_i - \alpha - \beta X_i)^2$$

with respect to α and β for a random sample $(X_1, Y_1), \ldots, (X_n, Y_n)$ are called the *least squares* as estimates of α_1^* and β_1^*. These estimates are universally known to be

$$\hat{\beta}_1^* = \sum_{i=1}^{n} (X_i - \bar{X})(Y_i - \bar{Y}) / \sum_{i=1}^{n} (X_i - \bar{X})^2 \qquad [4.6]$$

and $\quad \hat{\alpha}_1^* = \bar{Y} - \hat{\beta}_1^* \bar{X}.$

One might ask if a significant linear relationship exists between X and Y. The question can be answered affirmatively if the hypothesis H_o: $\beta_1^* = 0$ is rejected. We must make some assumptions about the distribution of $\hat{\beta}_1^*$ in order to proceed.

The usual assumptions are that Y has a normal distribution for each X and that the Xs are *known constants*, presumably under the control of the investigator. Under these assumptions, the statistic

$$T^* = \hat{\beta}_1^* / \hat{\sigma}(\hat{\beta}_1^*) \qquad [4.7]$$

obtained by dividing equation 4.6 by its estimated standard deviation, has a t distribution with $n - 2$ degrees of freedom under H_o.

Now suppose (X, Y) is some bivariate population, and let $Y|x$ be a random variable whose distribution is that of Y for a given value x of X; that is, the distribution of $Y|X$ is the conditional distribution of Y, given X. When X and Y are jointly normal, $Y|X$ is a normal random variable with mean

$$\mu_{Y|X} = \mu_Y + \frac{\rho \sigma_Y}{\sigma_X} (X - \mu_X) \qquad [4.8]$$

and variance $\sigma_{Y/X}^2 = \sigma_Y^2 (1 - \rho^2)$.

Among all predictors of Y in terms of X, it is known that the conditional mean of Y, given X, is the one with minimum mean squared predictive error. Since equations 4.2 and 4.8 are identical, the best linear predictor and the best overall predictor coincide in the normal case. It is for this reason that the normal distribution is so closely associated with least squares regression theory.

We have seen that the distribution of (X, Y) is concentrated on a line if $\rho^2 = 1$. Further, ρ ranges from -1 to 1, and if X and Y are independent, then $\rho = 0$. These properties hold regardless of whether or not (X, Y) has a bivariate normal distribution. However, $\rho = 0$ does not imply that X and Y are independent *unless* X and Y have a bivariate normal distribution.

Now, let $(X_1, Y_1), \ldots, (X_n, Y_n)$ be a sample from the bivariate population (X, Y). It is natural to estimate ρ with its sample analogue:

$$R = \frac{\sum_{i=1}^{n} (Y_i - \bar{Y})(X_i - \bar{X})}{\left[\sum_{i=1}^{n} (X_i - \bar{X})^2 \sum_{i=1}^{n} (Y_i - \bar{Y})^2 \right]^{1/2}} \quad [4.9]$$

For bivariate normal populations, equation 4.9 is the maximum likelihood estimator of ρ; it is the method-of-moments estimator of ρ for other distributions. Like ρ, R ranges from −1 to 1, inclusive.

What is the distribution of R? We consider this question only for samples from a bivariate normal population. As usual, there are two cases, depending on whether or not $\rho = 0$. If $\rho = 0$, the distribution of R is fairly easy to write down (see Morrison, 1976). It is more convient to work with the transformed variable

$$T = R \left(\frac{n - 2}{1 - R^2} \right)^{1/2} \quad [4.10]$$

than directly with R. When $\rho = 0$, equation 4.10 has Student's t distribution with n − 2 degrees of freedom. The hypothesis H_0: $\rho = 0$ can be tested against a suitable alternative by referring the computed value of T to tables of the t distribution with n − 2 degrees of freedom.[10]

When $\rho \neq 0$, the distribution of R is known (see Anderson, 1958), but it is too complicated to present here. Indeed, an approximation based on Fisher's "z transformation" is much more widely used. Fisher (1921) showed that the variable

$$Z = \frac{1}{2} \ln \frac{1 + R}{1 - R} \quad [4.11]$$

is distributed approximately as a normal variable with mean

$$\mu_Z \stackrel{\circ}{=} \frac{1}{2} \ln \frac{1 + \rho}{1 - \rho}$$

and variance

$$\sigma^2(Z) \stackrel{\circ}{=} 1/(n - 3)$$

Using equation 4.11, it is possible (1) to test hypotheses of the form H_o: $\rho = \rho_o$ (where $\rho_o \neq 0$) against suitable alternatives, (2) to establish confidence intervals for ρ, and (3) to compare values of R obtained from two independent multivariate normal samples. The interested reader is referred to Morrison (1976) for details and examples.

From equation 4.1, it would appear that ρ treats the variables X and Y symmetrically. However, the discussion of conditional distributions implies that one variable must be considered "independent" and the other "dependent." It turns out that for inferential purposes the view we adopt is immaterial. When $\rho = 0$, Fisher (1915) showed that the distribution of R is the same whether or not X is normal, provided only that Y is normal. Thus the fact that the statistics in equations 4.7 and 4.10 have the same distribution is no coincidence! (In other cases, the distribution of R *does* depend on X, however.)

We have seen that the correlation coefficient ρ has a number of desirable properties: (1) It ranges from -1 to 1, inclusive, (2) it is zero when X and Y are independent, and (3) it has a straightforward interpretation in terms of "proportion of variability explained" or "degree of linearity." In the normal case, (4) the estimator R has the same distribution when the underlying variables are treated symmetrically as when they are not, and (5) the distribution of R is known and easy to approximate. Finally, ρ characterizes the correlational structure between X and Y in the normal case because the regression of Y on X, or vice versa, is linear. In a sense, ρ is the prototype for other measures discussed in this monograph. All have been defined so as to preserve one or more properties of ρ in other contexts.

A discussion of correlation and regression theory can be found in any good elementary statistics textbook. A classical treatment is found in Snedecor and Cochran (1967). The distributional results involving R are given by Morrison (1976). The interpretation of ρ is given by Kruskal (1958).

Kendall's τ

Two pairs of observation (X_i, Y_i) and (X_j, Y_j) are said to be *concordant* if either $X_i < X_j$ and $Y_i < Y_j$ or $X_i > X_j$ and $Y_i > Y_j$; that is, the pairs are concordant if the larger of the two X values is paired with the larger Y value. Equivalently, the pairs are concordant if

$$(X_j - X_i)(Y_j - Y_i) > 0$$

The pairs are said to be *discordant* if the larger X value is paired with the smaller Y value, that is, if

$$(X_j - X_i)(Y_j - Y_i) < 0$$

Pairs for which

$$(X_j - X_i)(Y_j - Y_i) = 0$$

or pairs for which either $X_i = X_j$ or $Y_i = Y_j$ are said to be *tied*.

Let π_c, π_d, and π_t be the probabilities, respectively, that the two randomly selected pairs are concordant, discordant, or tied. In symbols, we have

$$\pi_c = P[X_j - X_i)(Y_j - Y_i) > 0] \qquad [4.12]$$

$$\pi_d = P[(X_j - X_i)(Y_j - Y_i) < 0] \qquad [4.13]$$

and

$$\pi_t = P[(X_j - X_i)(Y_j - Y_i) = 0] \qquad [4.14]$$

Two pairs of observations are necessarily concordant, discordant, or tied. Consequently, the probabilities (equations 4.12 through 4.14) must sum to one:

$$\pi_c + \pi_d + \pi_t = 1 \qquad [4.15]$$

Kendall's coefficient of concordance is defined by

$$\tau = \pi_c - \pi_d \qquad [4.16]$$

where π_c and π_d are given by equations 4.12 and 4.13, respectively. The coefficient τ is easy to interpret: If two observations (X_i, Y_i) and (X_j, Y_j) are selected at random from the population (X, Y), τ is the probability that they are concordant minus the probability that they are discordant.

If the population (X, Y) is continuous, $\pi_c + \pi_d = 1$ because $\pi = 0$ by assumption. Consequently, τ can range from -1 to 1. If X and Y are monotonically related,[11] $\tau = 1$ or $\tau = -1$, depending on whether the relationship is positive or negative. In particular, if the order of the population values when ranked according to X is the same as when they are ranked according to Y, $\tau = 1$. On the other hand, $\tau = -1$ if one ordering is the reverse of the other. When X and Y are independent, two observations are as likely to be discordant as concordant, so $\tau = 0$. The converse of the last statement need not be true: It is possible for τ to equal zero even though X and Y are not independent.

A natural estimator of τ is

$$\hat{\tau}_a = (C - D)/\binom{n}{2} = \frac{2(C - D)}{n(n - 1)}$$ [4.17]

where C is the number of concordant pairs, D is the number of discordant pairs, and $\binom{n}{2} = n(n - 1)/2$ is the total number of pairs of observations in a sample of size n. If the observations (X_i, Y_i) are arranged so that the Xs are in increasing order, the D turns out to be the minimum number of transpositions necessary to arrange the Ys in increasing order. For this reason, $\hat{\tau}_a$ is sometimes called a "coefficient of disarray."

Theoretically, $E(\hat{\tau}_a) = \tau$ for continuous populations, so $\hat{\tau}_a$ is an unbiased estimator of τ. Nevertheless, $\hat{\tau}_a$ is not a very good estimator of τ when ties are present in the data. The numerator of equation 4.17 is computed using only pairs that are not tied, while the denominator $\binom{n}{2}$ is the total number of pairs in the sample, both tied and otherwise. For this reason, $\hat{\tau}_a$ has a tendency to underestimate τ in the presence of ties.

Ideally, we would like an estimator in which the denominator, like the numerator, decreases as the proportion of ties in the sample increases. To get such an estimator, we must take a closer look at the ties. Consider a set of m observations that all have the same X value. There are $\binom{m}{2}$ pairs in this set, none of which is counted in computing C – D. The total number of pairs not counted in computing C – D because of tied X values is

$$U = \sum_i \binom{m_i}{2}$$ [4.18]

where m_i is the number of observations in the ith set of tied X values, and the sum extends over all sets of tied X values. Likewise, the total number of pairs not counted in computing C – D because of tied Y values is

$$V = \sum_j \binom{n_j}{2}$$ [4.19]

where n_j is the number of observations in the jth set of tied Y values, and the sum extends over all sets of tied Y values.

Starting with $\hat{\tau}_a$, it can be argued that we should decrease the denominator by U to compensate for tied Xs and by V to compensate for tied Ys. That is, the denominator of the estimator we seek should be a function of

$$\binom{n}{2} - U = \binom{n}{2} - \sum_i \binom{m_i}{2} \qquad [4.20]$$

and

$$\binom{n}{2} - V = \binom{n}{2} - \sum_j \binom{n_j}{2} \qquad [4.21]$$

The second estimator proposed by Kendall is obtained by replacing the denominator of equation 4.17 with the geometric mean of equations 4.20 and 4.21. The resulting estimator is

$$\hat{\tau}_b = \frac{C - D}{\left\{ \left[\binom{n}{2} - U \right] \left[\binom{n}{2} - V \right] \right\}^{1/2}}$$

$$= 2(C - D) / \left\{ [n(n-1) - 2U] [n(n-1) - 2V] \right\}^{1/2} \qquad [4.22]$$

where U and V are defined by equations 4.18 and 4.19, respectively.

The distinction between $\hat{\tau}_a$ and $\hat{\tau}_b$ is best illustrated by a simple example.

Example 3. Consider the following eight observations.

Observation	1	2	3	4	5	6	7	8
X	1	2	2	3	3	3	4	5
Y	1	3	2	1	5	3	4	5

It is easily verified that C = 18, D = 3. Moreover, $m_1 = 2$ (corresponding to the two values X = 2) and $m_2 = 3$ (corresponding to the three values X = 3); likewise $n_1 = n_2 = n_3 = 2$. Thus, $U = \binom{2}{2} + \binom{3}{2} = 4$ and $V = \binom{2}{2} \times 3 = 3$, so we have

$$\hat{\tau}_a = \frac{2(18 - 3)}{8 \times 7} = \frac{30}{56} = 0.536$$

and

$$\hat{\tau}_b = \frac{2(18 - 3)}{[(56 - 8)(56 - 6)]^{1/2}} = 0.612$$

Note that equations 4.17 and 4.22 both give the same value when there are no ties in the data.

In the absence of ties, both $\hat{\tau}_a$ and $\hat{\tau}_b$ range from a minimum value of -1 when all possible pairs are discordant to a maximum of $+1$ when all pairs are concordant. The ranges of both are restricted when ties are present, with the restriction for $\hat{\tau}_a$ being more severe. In all cases, $|\hat{\tau}_a| \leqslant |\hat{\tau}_b|$. There are cases, however, where the maximum achievable value of τ_b is strictly less than one even though all untied pairs are concordant.[12]

Now suppose that each X_i is replaced by its rank among the X values and suppose Y_i is similarly transformed, so the data consist of n pairs of ranks. The calculation of either $\hat{\tau}_a$ or $\hat{\tau}_b$ is unaffected by this transformation. If the data are ranks, $\hat{\tau}_a$ admits yet another interpretation. Consider a set of m tied ranks, and suppose that ties are broken by arbitrarily selecting one of the m! permutations of the set of tied values. (For example, if ranks 4 to 7 are tied, arbitrarily replace these values by one of the 4! = 24 permutations of $\{4, 5, 6, 7\}$.) If equation 4.17 or 4.22 is now calculated for each possible ordering and all values are averaged, the result is identical to that given by equation 4.17. Thus, $\hat{\tau}_a$ is the average of all values of τ_a or τ_b obtained by the assignment of integral ranks to sets of tied ranks in all possible ways.

If the data are rankings, Kendall (1970: 36-37) discusses the question of whether $\hat{\tau}_a$ or $\hat{\tau}_b$ is the more appropriate measure. Essentially, the choice depends on which is a better measure of *agreement* in the situation at hand. If the Xs and Ys represent ratings by two judges, then ties represent agreement and $\hat{\tau}_b$ should be used. If the Xs represent ratings by an individual, and the Ys represent a *known objective ordering*, then ties do not indicate agreement, and $\hat{\tau}_a$ is recommended.

What about the moments of $\hat{\tau}_a$ and $\hat{\tau}_b$? It has already been noted that

$$E(\hat{\tau}_a) = E(\hat{\tau}_b) = \tau$$

for any continuous bivariate population, so both estimators are unbiased. Moreover, for any continuous variates, it is known (see Gibbons, 1971: 211-213, for example) that

$$\sigma^2(\hat{\tau}_a) = \frac{1}{n(n-1)} [8\pi_c(1 - \pi_c) + 16(n - 2)(\pi_{cc} - \pi_c^2)] \qquad [4.23]$$

where π_{cc} is the probability that any one of three randomly selected observations is concordant with the other two. Note that $n^{1/2} \hat{\sigma}(\hat{\tau}_a) \to 16(\pi_{cc} - \pi_c^2)$ as $n \to \infty$.

In practice, it is necessary either to hypothesize or to estimate π_c and π_{cc}. If X and Y are independent, $\pi_c = 1/2$, and $\pi_{cc} = 5/18$, in which case equation 4.23 becomes

$$\sigma^2(\hat{\tau}_a) = (4n + 10)/[9n(n - 1)] \qquad [4.24]$$

In other cases, π_c and π_{cc} can be estimated from a sample by determining the number of concordant pairs and the number of triples in which one observation is concordant with the other two, respectively. When these estimates are substituted into equation 4.23, we get

$$\hat{\sigma}^2(\hat{\tau}_a) = \frac{16}{n^2(n-1)^2} \left[\sum_{i=1}^{n} C_i^2 - \frac{2(2n-3)}{n(n-1)} C^2 - C \right] \qquad [4.25]$$

where C_i is the total number of values in the sample concordant with (X_i, Y_i) and

$$\sum_{i=1}^{n} C_i = 2C$$

(because each pair is counted twice). An unbiased estimator is obtained by replacing the denominator in equation 4.25 with $n(n - 1)(n - 2)(n - 3)$. Unless n is rather large, equation 4.25 should be used with care, since it is possible to construct examples in which $\hat{\sigma}^2(\hat{\tau}_a)$ is negative for small values of n (Gibbons, 1971: 222).

The given variance formulas require modifications if the data contain ties. Only the case in which X and Y are independent is considered. If ties are present, a formula for the variance of $C - D$ is

$$\sigma^2(C - D) = \frac{1}{18} [n(n - 1)(2n + 5) - A_2 - B_2]$$

$$+ \frac{A_1 B_1}{9n(n - 1)(n - 2)} + \frac{2UV}{n(n - 1)} \qquad [4.26]$$

where

$$A_1 = \sum_i m_i(m_i - 1)(m_i - 2), B_1 = \sum_j n_j(n_j - 1)(n_j - 2)$$

$$A_2 = \sum_i m_i(m_i - 1)(2m + 5), \quad B_2 = \sum_j n_j(n_j - 1)(2n_j + 5)$$

$$U = \sum_i \binom{m_i}{2} \quad \text{and} \quad V = \sum_j \binom{n_j}{2}$$

All summations extend over all sets of ties of size m_i in the X values or over all sets of ties of size n_j in the Y values, whichever is appropriate. From equations 4.17, 4.22, and 4.26 we get the variance formulas

$$\hat{\sigma}_t^2(\hat{\tau}_a) = \sigma^2(C - D)/\binom{n}{2}^2 \qquad [4.27]$$

and

$$\hat{\sigma}_t^2(\hat{\tau}_b) = \sigma^2(C - D)/\left\{\left[\binom{n}{2} - U\right]\left[\binom{n}{2} - V\right]\right\} \qquad [4.28]$$

respectively, for the estimators $\hat{\tau}_a$ and $\hat{\tau}_b$. If the sample contains ties in only one variable (say X), then equation 4.26 simplifies to

$$\sigma^2(C - D) = \frac{1}{18}[n(n - 1)(2n + 5) - A_2] \qquad [4.29]$$

Example 3 (continued). It can be verified that $A_1 = 2 \times 1 \times 0 + 3 \times 2 \times 1 = 6$; $B_1 = 3(2 \times 1 \times 0) = 0$; $A_2 = 2 \times 1 \times 9 + 3 \times 2 \times 11 = 84$; and $B_2 = 3(2 \times 1 \times 9) = 54$. Upon substitution of these values into equation 4.26, we get

$$\sigma^2(C - D) = \frac{1}{18}(8 \times 7 \times 21 - 84 - 54) + 0 + \frac{2 \times 4 \times 3}{8 \times 7} = 58.095$$

which, when substituted into equations 4.27 and 4.28, gives $\hat{\sigma}_t^2(\hat{\tau}_a) = 58.095/\binom{8}{2}^2 = 0.07410$ and $\hat{\sigma}_t^2(\hat{\tau}_b) = 58.095/(24 \times 25) = 0.09683$ as estimates of the variances of $\hat{\tau}_a$ and $\hat{\tau}_b$, respectively. The value $\hat{\sigma}_t^2(\hat{\tau}_a) = 0.07410$ may be compared with the value $\hat{\sigma}^2(\hat{\tau}_a) = 0.08333$ obtained from equation 4.24.

We must know the appropriate percentage points of the distribution of either $\hat{\tau}_a$ or $\hat{\tau}_b$ in order to make inferences about τ. Several tables of the exact distribution of $\hat{\tau}_a$ (or $\binom{n}{2} \times \hat{\tau}_a$) have been published for the case in which X and Y are independent. One of the most extensive is given by Conover (1980), where $\binom{n}{2} \hat{\tau}_a$ is tabulated for $n = 4(1)40$. Others are given by Kendall (1970), Siegel (1956), and Owen (1962). The exact distribution of $\hat{\tau}_b$ is not tabulated because it depends on the observed configuration of ties in the data.

The normal distribution can be used to approximate the distributions of $\hat{\tau}_a$ and $\hat{\tau}_b$ for large samples since both estimates are asymptotically normal. The approximations are quite good even for moderate n because the distributions of $\hat{\tau}_a$ and $\hat{\tau}_b$ are symmetric if $\tau = 0$, and they rapidly become so with increasing n otherwise. When $\tau = 0$, Kendall suggests that the normal approximation is adequate for $n > 10$. Provided τ is not too close to one, we can use the normal approximation confidently with sample sizes in excess of 15 or 20. When computing variance estimates, it is important to note that formula 4.25 holds in general, but that formulas 4.26 through 4.29 hold only when X and Y are independent. Formulas 4.24 and 4.26 through 4.29 are suitable only for testing the null hypothesis H_o: $\tau = 0$. For testing other hypotheses about τ and for constructing confidence intervals, formula 4.25 should be used. In the event that one of the variables denotes "time," a test of H_o: $\tau = 0$ versus H_1: $\tau > 0$ or of H_o: $\tau = 0$ versus H_1 $\tau < 0$ may be interpreted as a test for trend.

Good references for further reading include Conover (1980), Hays (1963), Kendall (1970), Gibbons (1971: 209-224), and Noether (1967: 70-82). Kendall's book is definitive. It contains many examples and all of the results presented here. The treatments of Gibbons and Noether are more mathematically sophisticated than the others.

Spearman's Rank Correlation Coefficient

Starting with the product-moment correlation coefficient R, it is easy to derive Spearman's rank correlation coefficient. Suppose the sample values (X_i, Y_i) are replaced by ranks. If the ranks are used in formula 4.9 in place of the original data, the result is one version of the rank correlation coefficient. It is natural to regard the resulting value as an estimate of the population correlation coefficient. Unfortunately, it is not a good estimator of ρ and, in fact, turns out to be fairly difficult to interpret in terms of a meaningful population parameter. The rank correlation coefficient was first studied by Spearman (1904).

Let R_i denote the rank of X_i among the Xs and let S_i be defined similarly for Y. Then, by replacing X_i and Y_i in equation 4.9 by R_i and S_i, respectively, we get

$$\hat{\rho}_b = \frac{\sum_{i=1}^{n} (R_i - \bar{R})(S_i - \bar{S})}{\left[\sum_{i=1}^{n} (R_i - \bar{R})^2 \sum_{i=1}^{n} (S_i - \bar{S})^2\right]^{1/2}} \qquad [4.30a]$$

Several versions of equation 4.30a exist. Although all versions give the same value for a sample with no ties, they give different values when ties are present. Details are given here to aid the reader who is confused by the many formulas for a single measure, not all of which give the same result in all cases.

Suppose for the moment that there no ties in the data. Since

$$\sum_{i=1}^{n} R_i = \sum_{i=1}^{n} i = \frac{1}{2} n(n+1) = \sum_{i=1}^{n} S_i$$

and

$$\sum_{i=1}^{n} R_i^2 = \sum_{i=1}^{n} i^2 = \frac{1}{6} n(n+1)(2n+1) = \sum_{i=1}^{n} S_i^2$$

some algebra reveals that

$$\sum_{i=1}^{n} (R_i - \bar{R})^2 = \frac{1}{12} n(n^2 - 1) = \sum_{i=1}^{n} (S_i - \bar{S})^2 \qquad [4.31]$$

Substitution of equation 4.31 into 4.30a yields

$$\hat{\rho}_a = \frac{12 \sum_{i=1}^{n} (R_i - \bar{R})(S_i - \bar{S})}{n^3 - n}$$

$$= \frac{12 \sum_{i=1}^{n} R_i S_i}{n(n^2 - 1)} - \frac{3(n+1)}{n-1} \qquad [4.32a]$$

It is convenient to assume that the Xs are listed in increasing order, in which case $R_i = i$, and formula 4.32a can be simplified by replacing

$$\sum_{i=1}^{n} R_i S_i \quad \text{with} \quad \sum_{i=1}^{n} i S_i$$

Finally, let

$$D_i = R_i - S_i = (R_i - \bar{R}) - (S_i - \bar{S})$$

Then

$$\sum_{i=1}^{n} D_i^2 = \sum_{i=1}^{n} (R_i - \bar{R})^2 + \sum_{i=1}^{n} (S_i - \bar{S})^2 - 2 \sum_{i=1}^{n} (R_i - \bar{R})(S_i - \bar{S})$$

$$= \frac{1}{6} n(n^2 - 1) - 2 \sum_{i=1}^{n} (R_i - \bar{R})(S_i - \bar{S})$$

so yet another form of equation 4.30a is

$$\hat{\rho}_s = 1 - \frac{6 \sum_{i=1}^{n} D_i^2}{n(n^2 - 1)} \qquad [4.33]$$

There are two widely used modifications of $\hat{\rho}_s$ that take account of ties. Although different in appearance, these versions turn out to be algebraically equivalent to equations 4.30a and 4.32a. Let m_j denote the number of observations in the jth set of tied X ranks, and let n_j be defined similarly for the Y ranks. Suppose that each rank within a group of ties is replaced by the average of the ranks corresponding to the group (for example, if observations corresponding to the ranks 4, 5, 6, 7 are tied on X, then each observation in the group is assigned an X rank of 5.5). The effect of the group of m_j tied X ranks on the value ΣD_i^2 is to decrease it by $m_i(m_i^2 - 1)/12$ relative to its value *had there been no ties*. The total reduction in ΣD_i^2 from all the groups of tied ranks in both variables is $U + V$, where

$$U = \frac{1}{12} \Sigma_j m_j(m_j^2 - 1) \quad \text{and} \quad V = \frac{1}{12} \Sigma_j n_j(n_j^2 - 1)$$

If $U + V$ is added to ΣD_i^2 in equation 4.33, the result is

$$\hat{\rho}_a = 1 - \frac{6 \left(\sum_{i=1}^{n} D_i^2 + U + V \right)}{n(n^2 - 1)} \qquad [4.32b]$$

The estimator $\hat{\rho}_a$ is equivalent to $\hat{\tau}_a$ in the following sense: If one of equations 4.30a, 4.30b, 4.32a, 4.32b, or 4.33 is computed for each possible permutation of the ranks in the tied sets, and all resulting values are averaged, that average is equal to the value given by equation 4.32b.

Further, the denominator of equation 4.32b can be adjusted to compensate for ties. The denominator of equation 4.32b is effectively reduced by 12U because of tied X ranks and by 12V because of tied Y ranks relative to its value when ties are absent. Substitution of the geometric mean of these adjusted values into the denominator of equation 4.32b in place of $n^3 - n$ yields

$$\hat{\rho}_b = \frac{n(n^2 - 1) - 6\left(\sum_{i=1}^{n} D_i^2 + U + V\right)}{[n(n^2 - 1) - 12U]^{1/2} [n(n^2 - 1) - 12V]^{1/2}} \qquad [4.30b]$$

The estimator $\hat{\rho}_b$ is analogous to $\hat{\tau}_b$. Clearly, $|\hat{\rho}_a| \leq |\hat{\rho}_b|$ and $\hat{\rho}_a \leq \hat{\rho}_s$. All of equations 4.30a, 4.30b, 4.32a, 4.32b, and 4.33 yield the same value for a sample with no ties. When ties are present, equations 4.30a and 4.30b yield one value, 4.32a and 4.32b yield another, and 4.33 yields still a third value.

An example will help to show how the estimators $\hat{\rho}_s$, $\hat{\rho}_a$, and $\hat{\rho}_b$ compare.

Example 3 (continued). When the original data are replaced by ranks, we get

R_i	1	2.5	2.5	5	5	5	7	8
S_i	1.5	4.5	3	1.5	7.5	4.5	6	7.5
$D_i = R_i - S_i$	−.5	−2	−.5	3.5	−2.5	.5	1	.5

Here, $m_1 = 2$, $m_2 = 3$ and $n_1 = n_2 = n_3 = 2$, so $U = [2(2^2 - 1) + 3(3^2 - 1)]/12 = 2.5$ and $V = 3 \times [2(2^2 - 1)]/12 = 1.5$. Since $\Sigma D_i^2 = 24.5$, equation 4.33 yields $\hat{\rho}_s = 1 - 6(24.5)/(8 \times 63) = 0.7083$, equation 4.32b yields $\hat{\rho}_a = 1 - 6(24.5 + 2.5 + 1.5)/(8 \times 63) = 0.6607$, and equation 4.30b yields

$$\hat{\rho}_b = \frac{8 \times 63 - 6(24.5 + 2.5 + 1.5)}{[(8 \times 63 - 30)(8 \times 63 - 18)]^{1/2}} = 0.6938$$

The considerations dictating the choice between $\hat{\tau}_a$ and $\hat{\tau}_b$ also apply to the choice between $\hat{\rho}_a$ and $\hat{\rho}_b$. If the data represent rankings of items by two judges, then ties represent agreement, and $\hat{\rho}_b$ is appropriate. On the other hand, if one variable represents the ranking of items by an individual and the other represents a *known* objective ordering, $\hat{\rho}_a$ is more suitable. Moreover, in situations in which one of the variables represents time, $\hat{\rho}_a$ may be regarded as a measure of trend.

We have seen that $|\hat{\rho}_a|$ is smallest and $|\hat{\rho}_s|$ tends to be largest in a given sampling situation. But how do the ranges of the three estimators compare? Suppose again for a moment that there are no ties, and suppose also that the Xs are arranged in increasing order so that R_i = Rank (X_i) = i. If all observations are concordant (see the sections on Kendall's τ in this chapter) so that $Y_i < Y_j$ whenever $X_i < X_j$, then S_i = i for all i as well. In this case D_i = 0 for each i and $\hat{\rho}_s$ = 1. Conversely, if all pairs are discordant, the Ys are in decreasing order, and S_i = n + 1 − i. In the latter case,

$$\sum_{i=1}^{n} D_i^2 = \frac{1}{3} n(n^2 - 1)$$

so we can see that $\hat{\rho}_s$ = −1. Other assignments of Y ranks lead to values between the extremes just considered, so all three estimators can range from −1 to 1 in the absence of ties.

Now suppose that ties are present. Let q_1 be the number of *distinct* X values in the sample, let q_2 be the number of *distinct* Y values, and let $q = \min\{q_1, q_2\}$. The minimum possible value of $\hat{\rho}_s$ is approximately $2/q^2 - 1$. The maximum possible value of $\hat{\rho}_s$ is 1 when $\Sigma D_i^2 = 0$, but this happens only if the Xs and Ys exhibit identical patterns of ties. The maximum possible vlaue of $\hat{\rho}_a$ is $d/(n^3 - n)$, where d is the denominator of equation 4.30b. This value depends on the observed configuration of ties and is attained by $\hat{\rho}_a$ when $\hat{\rho}_b$ = 1.

The estimator $\hat{\rho}_b$ ranges from −1 to 1, inclusive. Since $\hat{\rho}_b$ is a correlation coefficient, its range is unaffected by ties. Consequently, $\hat{\rho}_b$ is frequently the estimator of choice. Once the data have been replaced by ranks, with tied observations being replaced by their average rank, the calculation of $\hat{\rho}_b$ is most easily accomplished by means of equation 4.30a.

Expressions for the moments of $\hat{\rho}_s$, $\hat{\rho}_a$, and ρ_b are actually quite simple in the case of independence. If X and Y are independent, then so are the ranks R_i and S_i. It follows from equation 4.32a that $E(\hat{\rho}_a)$ = 0. Moreover, $\hat{\rho}_s$ has mean $E(\hat{\rho}_s)$ = 0 and variance

$$\sigma^2(\hat{\rho}_s) = 1/(n - 1) \qquad\qquad [4.34]$$

When X and Y are independent. Similar calculations reveal that ρ_b has the same mean and variance as $\hat{\rho}_s$:

$$E(\hat{\rho}_b) = 0 \quad \text{and} \quad \sigma^2(\hat{\rho}_b) = 1/(n - 1) \qquad\qquad [4.35]$$

The variance of $\hat{\rho}_a$ is obtained from that of $\hat{\rho}_b$ by noting that the former is a constant multiple of the latter. Consequently,

$$\sigma^2(\hat{\rho}_a) = \frac{[n(n^2 - 1) - 12U]\,[n(n^2 - 1) - 12V]}{n^2(n^2 - 1)^2(n - 1)} \qquad [4.36]$$

Example 3 (continued). For these data, formulas 4.34 to 4.36 yield the values $\sigma^2(\hat{\rho}_s) = \sigma^2(\hat{\rho}_b) = 1/7 = 0.1429$ and

$$\sigma^2(\hat{\rho}_a) = \frac{[8 \times 63 - 12(2.5)]\,[8 \times 63 - 12(1.5)]}{7(8 \times 63)^2} = 0.1296$$

Percentage points of the distribution of $\hat{\rho}_s$ or one of its variants are needed to perform significance tests. Under the hypothesis of independence, the distributions of all three statistics are symmetric about zero, and all are approximately normal for sufficiently large sample sizes. A number of tables of the exact distribution of ρ_s (or ΣD_i^2) are available for small samples. Kendall (1970) tabulates ΣD_i^2 for $n \leqslant 13$. Other tables are given by Owen (1962), Siegel (1956), and Conover (1980). The distributions of $\hat{\rho}_a$ and $\hat{\rho}_b$ are not tabulated because they depend on the observed configuration of ties.

The distributions of equations 4.30a, 4.30b, 4.32a, 4.32b, and 4.33 are rather "jagged," so their normal approximations are not as good as for estimators of τ. This jaggedness is illustrated by Figure 4.2 of Kendall (1970), which shows the frequency distribution of ΣD_i^2 for $n = 8$.

Since $\hat{\rho}_b$ is the product-moment correlation calculated from ranks of the observed data, approximations to the distribution of R are also recommended for $\hat{\rho}_s$ by some authors. One of these approximations stems from the fact that $(n - 2)^{1/2} R / (1 - R^2)^{1/2}$ is distributed approximately as a t random variable with $n - 2$ degrees of freedom for large samples (Hays, 1964; Morrison, 1976) under the hypothesis of independence (see the first section of this chapter). Unless n is *extremely* large, this approximation can be quite inaccurate, especially if the number of ties is significant. It is generally advisable to use the normal approximations based on equations 4.34, 4.35, and 4.36 when exact tables are unavailable.

We now turn to the matter or finding an interpretation for the statistics we have discussed. The Spearman rank correlation coefficient does not estimate an easily defined population parameter. In particular, $\hat{\rho}_s$ and its variants are not good estimators of the population correlation coefficient

ρ. It turns out that the problem of defining a population parameter corresponding to $\hat{\rho}_s$ is closely related to that of determining the distribution of $\hat{\rho}_s$ when X and Y are not independent. Kruskal (1958) has provided the most natural interpretation we have.

Consider three independent observations (X_i, Y_i), (X_j, Y_j), and (X_k, Y_k) of (X, Y). Let π'_c denote the probability that *at least one* pair is concordant with the other two and let π'_d denote the probability that *at least one* pair is discordant with the other two. If (X, Y) has a continuous distribution, then $\pi'_d = 1 - \pi'_c$. Since

$$E(\hat{\rho}_s) = \frac{n-2}{n+1} (\pi'_c - \pi'_d) + \frac{3}{n+1} \tau \qquad [4.37]$$

Kruskal proposes that

$$\rho_s = \pi'_c - \pi'_d$$

be taken as the population analog of $\hat{\rho}_s$. In equation 4.37 τ denotes Kendall's τ, defined by equation 4.16. The parameter ρ_s is the difference between two probabilities: (1) The probability that at least one of three observations is concordant with the other two and (2) the probability that at least one is discordant with the other two. Except when X and Y are independent, $\hat{\rho}_s$ is clearly a biased estimator of ρ_s.

When X and Y are not independent, Hoeffding (1948) has shown that $\hat{\rho}_s$ is approximately normal for large samples. Estimates of the variance of ρ_s are too complicated to present here. The interested reader is referred to Hoeffding's paper (1948: 318-321) for details. The statistics $\hat{\rho}_a$ and ρ_b are also approximately normal for large samples, but results are still more complicated because the exact distributions depend on the observed configuration of ties.

An upper bound on the variance of $\hat{\rho}_s$ can be obtained by means of the inequality

$$\sigma^2(\hat{\rho}_s) \leqslant \frac{3}{n} (1 - \rho_s^2) \qquad [4.38]$$

The right-hand side of equation 4.38 can be approximated by using $\hat{\rho}_s$ to estimate ρ_s. The use of equation 4.38 is conservative in that it produces confidence intervals that are wider than those obtained from actual variance estimates. The difference can be quite large in some cases.

Further references include Hays (1963: 641-647, 651-652). Conover (1980), Kendall (1970), Gibbons (1971: 226-240), Kruskal (1958), and

Hoeffding (1948: esp. 318-321). Hays and Conover give a brief discussion of the properties of $\hat{\rho}_s$ together with several examples. Kendall's treatment of the rank correlation coefficient is most extensive, and Kruskal presents the derivation of ρ_s given here. Gibbons gives a concise derivation of the properties of $\hat{\rho}_s$ and Hoeffding shows that the distributions of $\hat{\rho}_s$ is approximately normal when X and Y are not independent. The last two references are much more mathematically sophisticated than the first four.

5. MEASURES OF ASSOCIATION FOR ORDINAL DATA

Kendall's τ was originally defined for continuous bivariate data, so any version of τ intended for ordinal data must take ties into account. Several versions of τ and three related measures are considered. Except for the way ties are handled, all the measures are quite similar. Notation for this chapter is established in the next section.

Ordinal variables may be inherently discrete, or they may result from categorizing the range of a continuous variable. In either case, the multinomial sampling model is appropriate.

Preliminaries

Suppose that two ordinal variables X and Y are sampled jointly, and that the resulting sample $(X_1, Y_1), \ldots, (X_n, Y_n)$ is classified into an I × J contingency table. Then p_{ij} is the probability that an arbitrary observation (X_k, Y_k) falls into cell (i, j) of the table; that is, p_{ij} is the probability that X_k falls into (row) category i and Y_k falls into (column) category j. The number of observations that fall into cell (i, j) is denoted by n_{ij}.

From equation 4.15, we know that two pairs of observations must be concordant, discordant, or tied. Further investigation reveals that ties can occur in several ways. Two observations (X_i, Y_i) and (X_j, Y_j) can be tied (1) on X only (i.e., $X_i = X_j$ and $Y_i \neq Y_j$) or (2) on Y only (i.e., $X_i \neq X_j$ and $Y_i = Y_j$), or (3) they can be tied on both X and Y (i.e., $X_i = X_j$ and $Y_i = Y_j$). Observations that are tied only on X fall into the same row of the table, pairs that are tied only on Y fall into the same column, and pairs that are tied on both X and Y fall into the same cell of the table. By the reasoning that led to formula 4.15, we see that

$$\pi_t = \pi_t^X + \pi_t^Y + \pi_t^{XY} \tag{5.1}$$

where

$$\pi_t^X = P(X_i = X_j \quad \text{and} \quad Y_i \neq Y_j) \tag{5.2}$$

$$\pi_t^Y = P(X_i \neq X_j \quad \text{and} \quad Y_i = Y_j) \tag{5.3}$$

and

$$\pi_t^{XY} = P(X_i = X_j \quad \text{and} \quad Y_i = Y_j) \tag{5.4}$$

From equations 4.15 and 5.1 we see that

$$\pi_c + \pi_d + \pi_t = \pi_c + \pi_d + \pi_t^X + \pi_t^Y + \pi_t^{XY} = 1 \tag{5.5}$$

How can we express the probabilities in equation 5.5 in terms of the cell probabilities p_{ij}? Further, how can these quantities be estimated from a given sample? Let π_{ij}^c be the probability that a randomly selected observation (X_k, Y_k) is concordant with one *in cell* (i, j), and let π_{ij}^d be the probability that two such members are discordant. In terms of the p_{ij}s, it is easy to see that

$$\pi_{ij}^c = \sum_{i'<i} \sum_{j'<j} p_{i'j'} + \sum_{i'>i} \sum_{j'>j} p_{i'j'} \tag{5.6}$$

and

$$\pi_{ij}^d = \sum_{i'<i} \sum_{j'>j} p_{i'j'} + \sum_{i'>i} \sum_{j'<j} p_{i'j'} \tag{5.7}$$

Now, the probability that two randomly selected members of the population are concordant is

$$\pi_c = \sum_{i=1}^{I} \sum_{j=1}^{J} p_{ij}\pi_{ij}^c \tag{5.8}$$

and the probability that they are discordant is

$$\pi_d = \sum_{i=1}^{I} \sum_{j=1}^{J} p_{ij}\pi_{ij}^d \tag{5.9}$$

Consider next the terms in equation 5.1. The probabilities that two randomly selected individuals are tied on (1) both X and Y. (2) X alone, and (3) Y alone are:

$$\pi_t^{XY} = \sum_{i=1}^{I} \sum_{j=1}^{J} p_{ij}^2 \qquad [5.10]$$

$$\pi_t^{X} = \sum_{i=1}^{I} p_{i+}^2 - \sum_{i=1}^{I} \sum_{j=1}^{J} p_{ij}^2 \qquad [5.11]$$

and

$$\pi_t^{Y} = \sum_{j=1}^{J} p_{+j}^2 - \sum_{i=1}^{I} \sum_{j=1}^{J} p_{ij}^2 \qquad [5.12]$$

respectively. Substitution of equations 5.10, 5.11, and 5.12 into equation 5.1 reveals that

$$\pi_t = \sum_{i=1}^{I} p_{i+}^2 + \sum_{j=1}^{J} p_{+j}^2 - \sum_{i=1}^{I} \sum_{j=1}^{J} p_{ij}^2 \qquad [5.13]$$

It is also useful to note that

$$\pi_c + \pi_d + \pi_t^{X} = 1 - \pi_t^{Y} - \pi_t^{XY} = 1 - \sum_{j=1}^{J} p_{+j}^2 \qquad [5.14]$$

and

$$\pi_c + \pi_d + \pi_t^{Y} = 1 - \pi_t^{X} - \pi_t^{XY} = 1 - \sum_{i=1}^{I} p_{i+}^2 \qquad [5.15]$$

Finally, we need suitable estimates of equations 5.6 through 5.15. We begin by computing the number[13] of concordant and discordant pairs C and D in the sample $(X_1, Y_1), \ldots, (X_n, Y_n)$.

Observations concordant with one in cell (i, j) are those in cells that lie either "northwest" or "southeast" of that cell. The number of such pairs is

$$C_{ij} = \sum_{i'<j} \sum_{j'<j} n_{i'j'} + \sum_{i'>i} \sum_{j'>j} n_{i'j'} \qquad [5.16]$$

By summing over all cells, we see that

$$2C = \sum_{i=1}^{I} \sum_{j=1}^{J} n_{ij} C_{ij} \qquad [5.17]$$

The factor 2 appears in equation 5.17 because each concordant pair is counted twice in the summation. This repetition can be eliminated by writing

$$C = \sum_{i=1}^{I} \sum_{j=1}^{J} n_{ij} C_{ij}^{*} \qquad [5.18]$$

where

$$C_{ij}^{*} = \sum_{i'>i} \sum_{j'>j} n_{i'j'} \qquad [5.19]$$

is the total number of observations "southeast" of cell (i, j). We could as well have taken C_{ij} to be the first term on the right side of equation 5.16.

Likewise,

$$2D = \sum_{i=1}^{I} \sum_{j=1}^{J} n_{ij} D_{ij} \qquad [5.20]$$

where

$$D_{ij} = \sum_{i'<i} \sum_{j'>j} n_{i'j'} + \sum_{i'>i} \sum_{j'<j} n_{i'j'} \qquad [5.21]$$

is the number of observations discordant with one in cell (i, j). Note that D_{ij} is the total number of observations in cells "northeast" or "southwest" of cell (i, j). Equivalently,

$$D = \sum_{i=1}^{I} \sum_{j=1}^{J} n_{ij} D_{ij}^{*} \qquad [5.22]$$

where

$$D_{ij}^{*} = \sum_{i'<i} \sum_{j'>j} n_{i'j'} \qquad [5.23]$$

is the total number of observations "northeast" of cell (i, j).

Next, we need expressions for the numbers of ties of various types in the sample. An observation in cell (i, j) is tied on both X and Y with all other observations in that cell. Summing over all cells, we obtain

$$2T_{XY} = \sum_{i=1}^{I} \sum_{j=1}^{J} n_{ij}(n_{ij} - 1) = \sum_{i=1}^{I} \sum_{j=1}^{J} n_{ij}^2 - n \qquad [5.24]$$

where T_{XY} is the total number of sample pairs tied on both X and Y.

An observation in cell (i, j) is tied only on X with all other observations in row i not in cell (i, j). Consequently, (twice) the total number of ties involving only X is

$$2T_X = \sum_{i=1}^{I} \sum_{j=1}^{J} n_{ij}(n_{i+} - n_{ij}) = \sum_{i=1}^{I} n_{i+}^2 - \sum_{i=1}^{I} \sum_{j=1}^{J} n_{ij}^2 \qquad [5.25]$$

Likewise,

$$2T_Y = \sum_{j=1}^{J} n_{+j}^2 - \sum_{i=1}^{I} \sum_{j=1}^{J} n_{ij}^2 \qquad [5.26]$$

is twice the total number of ties involving only Y.

Finally, we need analogues to equations 5.14 and 5.15. The total number of pairs in a sample of size n is $\binom{n}{2} = n(n - 1)/2$. Thus,

$$2(C + D + T_X + T_Y + T_{XY}) = n(n - 1) \qquad [5.27]$$

from which we obtain

$$2(C + D + T_X) = n(n - 1) - 2(T_Y + T_{XY}) = n^2 - \sum_{j=1}^{J} n_{+j}^2 \qquad [5.28]$$

and

$$2(C + D + T_Y) = n^2 - \sum_{i=1}^{I} n_{i+}^2 \qquad [5.29]$$

Kendall's τ_b

Kendall originally proposed his measure

$$\tau = \pi_c - \pi_d \qquad [5.30]$$

for continuous variables. The measure in equation 5.30 admits an easy interpretation: If two observations (X_i, Y_i) and (X_j, Y_j) are selected at random from the population, τ is the probability that the observations are concordant (X and Y have like ordering) minus the probability that they are discordant (X and Y have unlike ordering). Two estimators of τ are discussed in Chapter 4:

$$\hat{\tau}_a = (C - D)/\binom{n}{2} = \frac{2(C - D)}{n(n - 1)} \qquad [5.31]$$

and

$$\hat{\tau}_b = \frac{C - D}{\left\{[\binom{n}{2} - U]\ [\binom{n}{2} - V]\right\}^{1/2}}$$

$$= 2(C - D)/\left\{[n(n - 1) - 2U]\ [n(n - 1) - 2V]\right\}^{1/2} \qquad [5.32a]$$

The estimator $\hat{\tau}_b$ is designed to reduce the downward bias exhibited by equation 5.31 in the presence of ties.

Now, $\pi_t = 0$ for continuous populations, while $\pi_t > 0$ in the discrete case. Consequently, the range of τ in the discrete case is restricted relative to its maximum range in the continuous case. Moreover, the range of τ depends on π_t, so τ is not particularly suitable for discrete populations. Likewise, the estimator $\hat{\tau}_a$ is not widely used with discrete data.

On the other hand, the estimator $\hat{\tau}_b$ is widely used in the ordinal case. Moreover, formula 5.32a can be written in simpler form using the notation of contingency tables. The numerator of formula 5.32a is most easily calculated using equations 5.18 and 5.22. Furthermore, expressions for U and V in the denominator of formula 5.32a take a particularly convenient form. Note that the number of tied groups of Xs is I (the number of rows) and the number of tied observations in the ith group is n_{i+}. Thus, equation 4.18 can be written as

$$U = \sum_{i=1}^{I} \binom{n_{i+}}{2} = \frac{1}{2} \sum_{i=1}^{I} n_{i+}(n_{i+} - 1)$$

$$= \frac{1}{2} \left(\sum_{i=1}^{I} n_{i+}^2 - n \right) \qquad [5.33]$$

Likewise, the number of pairs of observations tied on Y is

$$V = \frac{1}{2} \left(\sum_{j=1}^{J} n_{+j}^2 - n \right) \qquad [5.34]$$

Using equations 5.33 and 5.34, the denominator of equation 5.32a can be written as

$$\left\{[n(n-1)-2U]\,[n(n-1)-2V]\right\}^{1/2}$$

$$= \left[\left(n^2 - \sum_{i=1}^{I} n_{i+}^2\right)\left(n^2 - \sum_{j=1}^{J} n_{+j}^2\right)\right]^{1/2}$$

from which we obtain the formula

$$\hat{\tau}_b = \frac{2(C-D)}{[(n^2 - \sum_i n_{i+}^2)\,(n^2 - \sum_j n_{j+}^2)]^{1/2}} \tag{5.32b}$$

Finally, from equations 5.28 and 5.29, we get yet another expression for $\hat{\tau}_b$:

$$\hat{\tau}_b = \frac{C-D}{[(C+D+T_X)\,(C+D+T_Y)]^{1/2}} \tag{5.32c}$$

Note that $C + D + T_X$ is the number of pairs of observations *not* tied on Y, and $C + D + T_Y$ is the number of pairs *not* tied on X: The denominator of equation 5.32c is the geometric mean of these two quantities. Formula 5.32c is the best for comparing the various ordinal measures related to τ, while formula 5.32b is better for computational purposes.

The range of τ is not restricted in the continuous case, so $\hat{\tau}_b$ is the preferred estimator because $\hat{\tau}_a$ tends to underestimate when the data contain ties. In the discrete case, where $\pi_t > 0$, $\hat{\tau}_b$ is not a good estimator of τ; indeed $\hat{\tau}_a$ may actually be better because the range of τ *is* restricted. The estimator $\hat{\tau}_b$ is in fact the maximum likelihood estimator of the quantity

$$\tau_b = \frac{\pi_c - \pi_d}{\left[\left(1 - \sum_{i=1}^{I} p_{i+}^2\right)\left(1 - \sum_{j=1}^{J} p_{+j}^2\right)\right]^{1/2}} \tag{5.35}$$

under the multinomial sampling model. In view of equations 5.14 and 5.15, $1 - \Sigma_i p_{i+}^2$ and $1 - \Sigma_j p_{+j}^2$ are the probabilities, respectively, that randomly selected members of the population are *not* tied on Y (do not fall in the same column) and are *not* tied on X (do not fall in the same row). The denominator of equation 5.35 is the geometric mean of these two probabilities. Unless $p_{i+}^2 = p_{+j}^2 = 0$ for all i and j (that is, unless X and Y are continuous), it is clear that $|\tau_b| < |\tau|$.

Provided not all observations fall in a single cell, τ_b is well defined. For a square table, τ_b ranges from -1 to 1, with $\tau_b = 1$ if all observations fall in the main diagonal and $\tau_b = -1$ when all observations fall in the diagonal running from lower left to upper right.[14] Otherwise, the range of τ_b is still somewhat restricted. In the case of independence, τ_b is zero regardless of whether or not the table is square. Similar statements hold for $\hat{\tau}_b$.

For I = J = 2, equation 5.35 can be written as

$$\tau_b = \frac{p_{11}p_{22} - p_{12}p_{21}}{(p_{1+}p_{+1}p_{2+}p_{+2})^{1/2}}$$

which together with equations 3.60 and 3.1 reveals that the correlation coefficient ρ and the coefficient of mean square contingency ϕ are all of equal magnitude.

Under the multinomial sampling model, $\hat{\tau}_b$ is asymptotically normal with mean $\hat{\tau}_b$ and variance $\sigma_\infty^2(\hat{\tau}_b)$. Let d_1 and d_2 denote the denote the expressions given by equations 5.28 and 5.29, respectively, and let d denote the denominator of equation 5.32. Clearly, $d = (d_1 d_2)^{1/2}$. Now, $\sigma_\infty^2(\hat{\tau}_b)$ can be estimated by means of the following formula:

$$\hat{\sigma}_\infty^2(\hat{\tau}_b) = \frac{1}{n^2} \sum_{i=1}^{I} \sum_{j=1}^{J} n_{ij}z_{ij}^2 - \frac{1}{n}\bar{z}^2 \qquad [5.36]$$

where

$$d^2 z_{ij} = 2nd(C_{ij} - D_{ij}) + n\hat{\tau}_b(n_{i+}d_1 + n_{+j}d_2) \qquad [5.37]$$

and

$$\bar{z} = \frac{1}{n} \sum_{i=1}^{I} \sum_{j=1}^{J} n_{ij}z_{ij}$$

In equation 5.37, C_{ij} and D_{ij} are given by equations 5.16 and 5.21, respectively. If X and Y are independent, $\tau_b = 0$ and equation 5.36 becomes

TABLE 4
Relationship Between Past and Expected Financial Well-Being
Among Voters in Senate Elections

Present Financial Well-Being (X)	Expected Financial Well-Being (Y)			Totals
	Better (1)	Same (2)	Worse (3)	
Better (1)	70	85	15	170
Same (2)	10	134	41	185
Worse (3)	27	60	100	187
Totals	107	279	156	542

SOURCE: Kuklinski and West (1981). Their source: 1978 National Election Study, Center for Political Studies, University of Michigan.

$$\hat{\sigma}^2_{\infty}(\hat{\tau}_b) = \frac{4}{d^2} \left[\sum_{i=1}^{I} \sum_{j=1}^{J} n_{ij}(C_{ij} - D_{ij})^2 - \frac{4}{n}(C - D)^2 \right] \qquad [5.38]$$

Formula 5.38 should be used to test the hypothesis $\tau_b = 0$, while formula 5.36 should be used to make all other inferences about τ.

Example 4. In a study of economic voting behavior, Kuklinski and West (1981) present the data in Table 4. The data were obtained by asking the following two questions of 542 individuals who voted in 1978 Senate elections: (1) Would you say you are better off, worse off, or about the same financially as you were a year ago? and (2) Do you expect to be better off, worse off, or about the same financially a year from now? One question of interest is how well voters' estimates of past and future financial well-being are correlated.

Values of C_{ij} and D_{ij} for the data in Table 4 are shown in Table 5. From equations 5.17 and 5.20, we obtain $2C = 100,870$ and $2D = 27,590$. Thus,

$$\hat{\tau}_a = \frac{2(C - D)}{n(n - 1)} = \frac{73,280}{293,222} = 0.250$$

and

$$\hat{\tau}_b = 73,280 / [(542^2 - 170^2 - 185^2 - 187^2) \times$$

$$(542^2 - 107^2 - 279^2 - 156^2)]^{1/2}$$

$$= 0.390$$

From equations 5.36 and 5.37 we get $\hat{\sigma}_\infty(\hat{\tau}_b) = (0.0014015)^{1/2} = 0.0374$ as the estimated large-sample standard deviation of $\hat{\tau}_b$. As one would expect, any reasonable confidence interval for $\hat{\tau}_b$ does not contain zero. Had our only interest been in testing the hypothesis $\tau_b = 0$, the value $\hat{\sigma}_\infty(\hat{\tau}_b) = (0.0014872)^{1/2} = 0.0386$ from equation 5.38 should be used in place of the value 0.0374.

The interested reader can verify that $\hat{\kappa} = 0.338$ is the value of Cohen's measure of agreement for these data. Even though past and expected financial well-being are highly correlated, the agreement between them is perhaps not as high as one might expect.

Properties of $\hat{\tau}_b$ for continuous variables are discussed in Chapter 4. Formulas 5.37 and 5.38 are given by Agresti (1976) and by Brown and Benedetti (1977). Additional examples are presented by Hays (1963), Blalock (1972), and Reynolds (1977a). Wilson (1969) has provided a proportional-reduction-in-predictive-error interpretation for τ_b.

Measures Related to Kendall's τ_b

THE KENDALL-STUART τ_c

The measure τ_b and its estimator $\hat{\tau}_b$ cannot attain the extreme values +1 or −1 for tables that are not square. Following Kendall, Stuart (1953) proposes an estimator whose range is less restricted. Stuart's estimator is obtained by dividing the numerator of $\hat{\tau}_b$ by its maximum possible value. The maximum value of $2(C - D)$ is attained if all observations fall in an (longest) upper left to lower right diagonal of length $q = \min\{I, J\}$ and all frequencies are equal. In this case, n is a multiple of q, $D = 0$, and we can see from equation 5.17 that 2C has the value

$$2\left(\frac{n}{q}\right)\left[(q-1)\,\frac{n}{q}\,+(q-2)\,\frac{n}{q}\,+\ldots+\,\frac{n}{q}\right] = n^2(q-1)/q \qquad [5.39]$$

Even if n is not a multiple of q, this maximum (equation 5.39) is nearly attained for large n and (relatively) small q. In view of equation 5.39, Stuart takes

$$\hat{\tau}_c = 2(C - D)/[n^2(q - 1)/q] = \frac{2q(C - D)}{n^2(q - 1)} \qquad [5.40]$$

as an estimator of τ_b. Clearly

TABLE 5
Values of C_{ij} and D_{ij} for Data in Table 4

i \ j	C_{ij} 1	2	3	i \ j	D_{ij} 1	2	3
1	335	141	0	1	0	37	231
2	160	170	155	2	100	42	87
3	0	80	299	3	275	56	0

$$\hat{\tau}_c = \frac{n-1}{n} \; \frac{q}{q-1} \; \hat{\tau}_a \qquad [5.41]$$

and we can see that

$$|\hat{\tau}_a| \leqslant |\hat{\tau}_c| \leqslant |\hat{\tau}_b| \quad \text{for } n \geqslant q. \quad \text{When } I = J = 2,$$

$$\hat{\tau}_c = \frac{4}{n^2} \, (n_{11} n_{22} - n_{21} n_{12})$$

which shows that $\hat{\tau}_c$ is a function of the cross-product ratio in fourfold tables.
Since $\hat{\tau}_a$ is an unbiased estimator of τ, we have

$$E(\hat{\tau}_c) = \frac{n-1}{n} \; \frac{q}{q-1} \; \tau$$

Consequently, $\hat{\tau}_c$ is an asymptotically unbiased estimator of

$$\tau_c = \frac{q}{q-1} \, \tau$$

a quantity that may bear little relationship to τ_b. Under the multinominal model, $\hat{\tau}_c$ is approximately normal for large n. The estimated variance of τ_c is

$$\hat{\sigma}_\infty^2(\hat{\tau}_c) = \frac{4}{n^4} \left(\frac{q}{q-1}\right)^2 \left[\sum_{i=1}^{I} \sum_{j=1}^{J} n_{ij}(C_{ij} - D_{ij})^2 \right.$$

$$-\frac{4}{n}(C-D)^2\Bigg] \tag{5.42}$$

The coefficient of $C - D$ in equation 5.40 is a constant, so equation 5.42 is also correct under the hypothesis of independence. It is apparent from equation 5.41 that the difference between $\hat{\tau}_c$ and $\hat{\tau}_a$ increases as q decreases. The dependence of $\hat{\tau}_c$ on the dimensions of the table makes it difficult to interpret, especially if the cageories result from collapsing the range of an underlying continuous variable. Somers (1962b: 809) states that $\hat{\tau}_c$ is "a normed version of a product-moment analogue . . . unlikely to yield a useful interpretation." The value of $\hat{\tau}_a$ decreases as the number of categories decreases and $\hat{\tau}_c$ compensates somewhat. Goodman and Kruskal (1959: 141) argue that such adjustment may be inappropriate since "it could well be the case that a finer cross classification would show that *within* the original cells a complete association did not exist."

Example 4 (continued). From equation 5.41, we see that

$$\hat{\tau}_c = \frac{541}{542} \frac{3}{2} \hat{\tau}_a = 0.374$$

for the data in Table 4. The values of $\hat{\tau}_c$ and $\hat{\tau}_b$ are quite similar in this case. From equation 5.42, the estimated large-sample standard deviation of $\hat{\tau}_c$ is $\hat{\sigma}_\infty(\hat{\tau}_c) = (0.0013668)^{1/2} = 0.0370$.

The estimator $\hat{\tau}_c$ is discussed by Stuart (1953), Kendall (1970), and Goodman and Kruskal (1954). Goodman and Kruskal give a brief comparison of the behavior of $\hat{\tau}_c$ and $\hat{\gamma}$ (discussed below).

THE GOODMAN-KRUSKAL γ

The Goodman-Kruskal γ is another widely used measure that is closely related to Kendall's τ. This measure is defined by

$$\gamma = \frac{\pi_c - \pi_d}{1 - \pi_t} = \frac{\pi_c - \pi_d}{\pi_c + \pi_d} = \frac{\tau}{\pi_c + \pi_d} \tag{5.43a}$$

With the aid of equations 5.8, 5.9, and 5.13, γ can be written as

$$\gamma = \frac{\pi_c - \pi_d}{1 - \sum_{i=1}^{I} p_{i+}^2 - \sum_{j=1}^{J} p_{+j}^2 + \sum_{i=1}^{I} \sum_{j=1}^{J} p_{ij}^2}$$

Note that $\gamma = \tau = \tau_b$ if $\tau_t = 0$, while $|\gamma| \geqslant |\tau_b| \geqslant |\tau|$ otherwise. Consequently, γ has the same interpretation conditionally that τ has unconditionally: γ is the conditional probability that a pair of observations selected at random from the population are concordant minus the probability that they are discordant, the condition being that the pairs are not tied on either variable.

Unless the population is concentrated in a single row or column of the table, γ is well defined. The measure ranges from -1 to 1, inclusive, assuming the value 1 for a population that lies entirely in an (longest) upper left to lower right diagonal and the value -1 for a population that falls in a lower left to upper right diagonal. If X and Y are independent, $\gamma = 0$, but the converse need not be true.

The maximum likelihood estimator of γ under the multinomial sampling model is

$$\hat{\gamma} = \frac{C - D}{C + D} = \frac{2(C - D)}{n^2 - \sum\limits_{i=1}^{I} n_{i+}^2 - \sum\limits_{j=1}^{J} n_{+j}^2 + \sum\limits_{i=1}^{I} \sum\limits_{j=1}^{J} n_{ij}^2} \qquad [5.44]$$

where C and D are most easily calculated from equations 5.18 and 5.19 and 5.22 and 5.23, respectively. The estimator (equation 5.44) is well defined except when all observations fall in a single row or column of the table. The range of $\hat{\gamma}$ is identical to that of γ. If $\gamma = 1$ (or -1), it follows that $\hat{\gamma} = 1$ (or -1) also. On the other hand, it is possible to have $\hat{\gamma} = 1$ (or -1) even though $\gamma \neq 1$ (or -1). Just as $|\gamma| \geqslant |\tau_b|$, it is evident from equations 5.44 and 5.32c that $|\hat{\gamma}| \geqslant |\hat{\tau}_b|$. Finally Yule's Q is identical to the Goodman-Kruskal γ for fourfold tables. Unlike $\hat{\tau}_a$, $\hat{\tau}_b$, and $\hat{\tau}_c$, $\hat{\gamma}$ can achieve its extreme values of $+1$ or -1 in the cases of weak perfect positive or negative correlation.[15]

Under the multinomial sampling model, γ is asymptotically normal with mean $E(\gamma) = \gamma$ and variance

$$\sigma_\infty^2(\hat{\gamma}) = \frac{16}{n(1 - \pi_t)^4} \sum_{i=1}^{I} \sum_{j=1}^{J} p_{ij} [\pi_c \pi_{ij}^d - \pi_d \pi_{ij}^c]^2 \qquad [5.45]$$

where π_{ij}^d and π_{ij}^c are given by equations 5.7 and 5.6. The quantities π_{ij}^d and π_{ij}^c are the probabilities that a randomly selected observation is discordant or concordant, respectively, with a given observation in cell (i, j). Recall from equations 5.8 and 5.9 that π_c and π_d are the probabilities that two pairs of randomly selected observations are concordant or discordant, respectively.

An estimator of equation 5.45 is obtained by replacing π_c, π_d, and so on with their sample analogues:

$$\hat{\sigma}^2_\infty(\hat{\gamma}) = \frac{4}{(C+D)^4} \sum_{i=1}^{I} \sum_{j=1}^{J} n_{ij}(DC_{ij} - CD_{ij})^2 \qquad [5.46]$$

In equation 5.46, C_{ij}, C, D_{ij}, and D are given respectively by equations 5.16, 5.18, 5.21, and 5.22.

Under the hypothesis of independence, γ equals zero. For this case, Brown and Benedetti (1977) give the formula

$$\hat{\sigma}^2_\infty(\hat{\gamma}) = \left[\sum_{i=1}^{I} \sum_{j=1}^{J} n_{ij}(C_{ij} - D_{ij})^2 - \frac{4}{n}(C-D)^2 \right] / (C+D)^2 \qquad [5.47]$$

As usual, equation 5.46 should be used for all inferences except testing the hypothesis $\gamma = 0$, in which case equation 5.47 should be used.

When $\pi_t = 0$, equation 5.45 reduces to $16(\pi_{cc} - \pi_c^2)/n$, where π_{cc} is defined as in equation 4.23. Taken together, these results show that $\hat{\tau}_a$ and $\hat{\gamma}$ have the same asymptotic variances. This is as it should be, since $\hat{\gamma}$ and $\hat{\tau}_a$ are equal when $\pi_t = 0$.

Example 4 (continued). For the data in Table 4 we get

$$\hat{\gamma} = \frac{C-D}{C+D} = \frac{50{,}435 - 13{,}795}{50{,}435 + 13{,}795} = \frac{36{,}460}{64{,}230} = 0.570$$

Note that this value is considerably larger than the values of $\hat{\tau}_a$, $\hat{\tau}_b$, and $\hat{\tau}_c$. When the underlying variables are continuous, results of Agresti (1976) indicate that $\hat{\gamma}$ tends to overestimate γ, especially when I and J are small. From equation 5.46, the estimated large-sample standard deviation of $\hat{\gamma}$ is $\hat{\sigma}_\infty(\hat{\gamma}) = (0.0025616)^{1/2} = 0.0506$, while equation 5.47 yields $\hat{\sigma}_\infty(\hat{\gamma}) = (0.0031767)^{1/2} = 0.0564$. From either, it is certainly safe to conclude that $\gamma \neq 0$.

Properties of $\hat{\gamma}$ are given in three papers by Goodman and Kruskal (1954, 1963, 1972) and one by Brown and Benedetti (1977). Formula 5.47 is given by Brown and Benedetti. Together with another form of equation 5.46, Goodman and Kruskal give several numerical examples. Additional numerical examples are given by Hays (1963) and Reynolds (1977a).

SOMERS'S d

The measures proposed by Somers are closely related to τ, but unlike similiar measures, they do not treat X and Y symmetrically. There are actually two measures depending on which variable plays the role of "independent" variable.

Recall that π_t^X is the probability that two randomly selected observations are tied only on X and π_t^{XY} is the probability that they are tied on both X and Y. Then the probability that the two observations are tied on X *without regard to Y* is $\pi_t^X + \pi_t^{XY}$.

Now, Somers's measure $d_{Y \cdot X}$ is defined by

$$d_{Y \cdot X} = \frac{\pi_c - \pi_d}{1 - \pi_t^X - \pi_t^{XY}} \qquad [5.48a]$$

In view of equations 4.15 and 5.1, equation 5.48a can be written as

$$d_{Y \cdot X} = \frac{\pi_c - \pi_d}{\pi_c + \pi_d + \pi_t^Y} \qquad [5.48b]$$

and from equation 5.15, it follows that

$$d_{Y \cdot X} = \frac{\pi_c - \pi_d}{1 - \sum_{i=1}^{I} p_{i+}^2} \qquad [5.48c]$$

The first version of equation 5.48 is easiest to interpret, the second is useful for comparing $d_{Y \cdot X}$ to other measures, and the third is convenient for computational purposes.

From equation 5.48a, it is clear that $d_{Y \cdot X}$ has an interpretation similar to γ. The measure $d_{Y \cdot X}$ is the difference between two conditional probabilities, the conditional probability that two randomly selected observations are concordant minus the conditional probability that they are discordant, the condition in both cases being that the observations do not have the same X value. Let the two observations be (X_i, Y_i) and (X_j, Y_j). Then, in symbols, $d_{Y \cdot X}$ is the difference in the probabilities of the events that $(Y_i - Y_j)(X_i - X_j) > 0$ and $(X_i - Y_j)(X_i - X_j) < 0$, both probabilities being conditional on the event that $X_i \neq X_j$.

When $I = J = 2$, equation 5.48 reduces to

$$d_{Y \cdot X} = \frac{P_{11}P_{22} - P_{21}P_{12}}{P_{1+}P_{2+}} = \frac{P_{11}}{P_{1+}} - \frac{P_{21}}{P_{2+}} \quad [5.49]$$

From equation 5.49, we see that in a fourfold table, $d_{Y \cdot X}$ is simply the difference between the probability that $Y = 1$, given $X = 1$, and the probability that $Y = 1$, given $X = 2$ (where the levels of X and Y identify the rows and columns of the table).

By interchanging the roles of X and Y, we obtain the measure

$$d_{X \cdot Y} = \frac{\pi_c - \pi_d}{1 - \pi_t^Y - \pi_t^{XY}} = \frac{\pi_c - \pi_d}{\pi_c + \pi_d + \pi_t^X} = \frac{\pi_c - \pi_d}{1 - \sum\limits_{j=1}^{J} p_{+j}^2} \quad [5.50]$$

In the 2 × 2 case, equation 5.50 reduces to

$$d_{X \cdot Y} = \frac{P_{11}P_{22} - P_{21}P_{12}}{P_{+1}P_{+2}} = \frac{P_{11}}{P_{+1}} - \frac{P_{12}}{P_{+2}} \quad [5.51]$$

Interpretations of equation 5.50 and 5.51 are completely analogous to those of 5.48 and 5.49, respectively.

The measure $d_{Y \cdot X}$ is well defined unless the entire population falls into a single row of the table, while $d_{X \cdot Y}$ is well defined if the population does not fall into a single column of the table; both are well defined if the table of population probabilities has nonzero entries in at least two rows and two columns. Both $d_{X \cdot Y}$ and $d_{Y \cdot X}$ are zero when X and Y are independent, although the converse need not hold (except for 2 × 2 tables) in either case. Both $d_{X \cdot Y}$ and $d_{Y \cdot X}$ can range from −1 to 1. In a square table, $d_{X \cdot Y} = d_{Y \cdot X} = 1$ when the entire population falls in the main diagonal, while both measures equal −1 if the population falls entirely in the diagonal extending from lower left to upper right. It is also possible for $d_{Y \cdot X}$ to assume the extreme values ±1 in tables that are not square. Provided each column has a single nonzero entry, $|d_{Y \cdot X}|$ can equal 1 even though one or more rows contain multiple nonzero entries. This is so because observations tied on X do not enter into the definition of $d_{Y \cdot X}$. Likewise, $|d_{X \cdot Y}|$ can equal 1 provided each row of the table has a single nonzero entry.

How do $d_{X \cdot Y}$ and $d_{Y \cdot X}$ compare to the other "τ-like" measures? Clearly, $|d_{X \cdot Y}| \leqslant |\gamma|$ and $|d_{Y \cdot X}| \leqslant |\gamma|$. Also, $|d_{X \cdot Y}| \geqslant |e|$ and $|d_{Y \cdot X}| \geqslant |e|$, where e denotes Wilson's e. Further, $\gamma = d_{Y \cdot X}$ and $d_{X \cdot Y} = e$ if $\pi_t^Y = 0$, while $\gamma = d_{X \cdot Y}$ and $d_{Y \cdot X} = e$ when $\pi_t^X = 0$.

It is apparent from equations 5.48c, 5.50, and 5.35 that $d_{X \cdot Y} \times d_{Y \cdot X} = \tau_b^2$. Thus, τ_b is the geometric mean between Somers's two measures. All three measures are equal when $\pi_t^Y = 0$.

Somers (1962b) has shown that $\tau_c \leqslant d_{X \cdot Y}$. Equality holds when $I < J$ and the X-marginal (row) probabilities are all equal. Analogous relationships hold between τ_c and $d_{Y \cdot X}$.

By analogy with the Goodman-Kruskal measures of proportional reduction in predictive error, a symmetric version of somers's d can be defined (Nie et al., 1975: 229):

$$d = \frac{(\pi_c + \pi_d + \pi_t^X) d_{X \cdot Y} + (\pi_c + \pi_d + \pi_t^Y) d_{Y \cdot X}}{(\pi_c + \pi_d + \pi_t^X) + (\pi_c + \pi_d + \pi_t^Y)}$$

$$= \frac{\pi_c - \pi_d}{2 - \sum_{i=1}^{I} p_{i+}^2 + \sum_{j=1}^{J} p_{+j}^2}$$

The measure d is suitable when one of X or Y is arbitrarily selected a priori to play the role of the independent variable; d is well defined when the table of population probabilities has nonzero entries in at least two rows and columns. Clearly, d must be intermediate in value between $d_{X \cdot Y}$ and $d_{Y \cdot X}$.

The maximum likelihood estimator of $d_{Y X}$ under the multinomial sampling model is

$$\hat{d}_{Y \cdot X} = \frac{C - D}{C + D + T_Y} \qquad [5.52a]$$

where C, D, and T_Y are given respectively by equations 5.18, 5.22, and 5.26. In view of equation 5.29, 5.52a can be written as

$$\hat{d}_{Y \cdot X} = \frac{2(C - D)}{n^2 - \sum_{i=1}^{I} n_{i+}^2} \qquad [5.52b]$$

Likewise, the maximum likelihood estimators of $d_{X \cdot Y}$ and d are

$$\hat{d}_{X \cdot Y} = \frac{C - D}{C + D + T_X} = \frac{2(C - D)}{n^2 - \sum\limits_{j=1}^{J} n_{+j}^2}$$

and

$$\hat{d} = \frac{2(C - D)}{n^2 - \frac{1}{2}\left(\sum\limits_{i=1}^{I} n_{i+}^2 + \sum\limits_{j=1}^{J} n_{+j}^2\right)} = \frac{4(C - D)}{2n^2 - \sum\limits_{i=1}^{I} n_{i+}^2 - \sum\limits_{j=1}^{J} n_{+j}^2}$$

Statements about when $\hat{d}_{Y \cdot X}$ and $\hat{d}_{X \cdot Y}$ and d are well defined, about their extreme values, and about their relationships with (estimators of) other measures follow verbatim from those already made about their respective population analogues.

All three estimators have asymptotically normal distributions under the multinomial sampling model. Goodman and Kruskal (1972) give the following expression for the asymptotic variance of $\hat{d}_{Y \cdot X}$:

$$\sigma_\infty^2(\hat{d}_{Y \cdot X}) = \frac{4}{n\delta^2} \sum\limits_{i=1}^{I} \sum\limits_{j=1}^{J} p_{ij}[\nu(1 - p_{i+}) - \delta(\pi_{ij}^c - \pi_{ij}^d)]^2 \qquad [5.53]$$

where

$$\nu = \pi_c - \pi_d \quad \text{and} \quad \delta = 1 - \sum\limits_{i=1}^{I} p_{i+}^2$$

are the numerator and denominator of $d_{Y \cdot X}$. The sample analogue of equation 5.53 serves as an estimator: An algebraically convenient form of the estimator is

$$\hat{\sigma}_\infty^2(\hat{d}_{Y \cdot X}) = \frac{4}{n^4(n + n_{i+})^2} \sum\limits_{i=1}^{I} \sum\limits_{j=1}^{J} n_{ij}[2(C - D)$$

$$- (n + n_{i+})(C_{ij} - D_{ij})]^2 \qquad [5.54]$$

If $d_{Y \cdot X} = 0$, the estimated variance of $\hat{d}_{Y \cdot X}$ becomes

$$\hat{\sigma}_\infty^2(\hat{d}_{Y \cdot X}) = \frac{4\left[\sum\limits_{i=1}^{I} \sum\limits_{j=1}^{J} n_{ij}(C_{ij} - D_{ij})^2 - \dfrac{4}{n}(C - D)^2\right]}{\left(n^2 - \sum\limits_{i=1}^{I} n_{i+}^2\right)^2} \qquad [5.55]$$

As usual, equation 5.55 should be used to test the hypothesis $d_{Y \cdot X} = 0$, and equation 5.54 should be used otherwise.

Variance formulas for $\hat{d}_{X \cdot Y}$ can be obtained from those for $\hat{d}_{Y \cdot X}$ by symmetry. Corresponding to equations 5.54 and 5.55, we have

$$\hat{\sigma}_\infty^2(\hat{d}_{X \cdot Y}) = \frac{4}{n^4(n + n_{+j})^2} \sum\limits_{i=1}^{I} \sum\limits_{j=1}^{J} n_{ij}[2(C - D)$$

$$- (n + n_{+j})(C_{ij} - D_{ij})]^2$$

and

$$\hat{\sigma}_\infty^2(\hat{d}_{X \cdot Y}) = \frac{4\left[\sum\limits_{i=1}^{I} \sum\limits_{j=1}^{J} n_{ij}(C_{ij} - D_{ij})^2 - \dfrac{4}{n}(C - D)^2\right]}{\left(n^2 - \sum\limits_{j=1}^{J} n_{+j}^2\right)^2}$$

The method of Example 2 can be used to approximate the variance of $\hat{d}$.

Example 4 (continued). For the data in Table 4, we obtain

$$\hat{d}_{Y \cdot X} = \frac{2(C - D)}{n^2 - \sum\limits_{i=1}^{I} n_{i+}^2} = \frac{2 \times 36{,}640}{542^2 - 170^2 - 185^2 - 187^2}$$

$$= \frac{73{,}280}{195{,}670} = 0.375$$

$$\hat{d}_{X \cdot Y} = \frac{2 \times 36{,}640}{542^2 - 107^2 - 279^2 - 156^2} = \frac{73{,}280}{180{,}138} = 0.407$$

and

$$\hat{d} = \frac{4 \times 36,640}{180,138 + 195,670} = \frac{146,560}{375,808} = 0.390$$

Notice that

$$\hat{d}_{Y \cdot X} \times \hat{d}_{X \cdot Y} = \frac{(73,280)^2}{180,138 \times 195,670} = \hat{\tau}_b^2$$

as indicated earlier. Calculation of the variance estimates (equations 5.54 and 5.55) is left as an exercise for the interested reader.

Somers introduced the asymmetric measures $d_{Y \cdot X}$ and $d_{X \cdot Y}$, and three of his papers (1962a, 1962b, 1968) contain discussions of their properties. A proportional-reduction-in-predictive-error interpretation similar to that for the Goodman-Kruskal τ is given in the 1968 paper. Formula 5.53 is given by Goodman and Kruskal (1972), and additional examples are found in Reynolds (1977a).

WILSON'S e

The last of the measures closely related to τ_b is symmetric. It differs from τ_b and γ in that only pairs of observations tied on both variables are considered irrelevant. Recall that π_t^{XY} is the probability that randomly selected pairs of observations are tied on both X and Y. Whereas γ is defined by ignoring all ties, Wilson's e is defined by ignoring only ties involving both X and Y. Thus

$$e = \frac{\pi_c - \pi_d}{1 - \pi_t^{XY}} = \frac{\pi_c - \pi_d}{\pi_c + \pi_d + \pi_t^X \pi_t^Y} = \frac{\pi_c - \pi_d}{1 - \sum_{i=1}^{I} \sum_{j=1}^{J} p_{ij}^2}$$

Interpretation of e is similar to that of γ and Somers's measures. When two members of the population are selected at random, e is the conditional probability that the pairs are concordant minus the conditional probability that they are discordant, the condition in each case being that the pairs are not tied on both X and Y. Precisely, e is the difference in the probabilities of the event that $(X_i - X_j)(Y_i - Y_j) > 0$ and the event that $(X_i - X_j)(Y_i - Y_j) < 0$, where both probabilities are conditional upon the event that at least one of $(X_i - X_j)$ or $(Y_i - Y_j)$ is not zero.

The measure e is well defined unless the entire population falls in a single cell, and e = 0 when X and Y are independent. It is clear that $|e|$ does not exceed the magnitude of any of the four related measures, τ_b, γ, $d_{Y \cdot X}$ and $d_{X \cdot Y}$. Moreover, $e = d_{X \cdot Y}$ when $\pi_t^Y = 0$ and $e = d_{Y \cdot X}$ when $\pi_t^X = 0$. All five measures are equal when both $\pi_t^X = 0$ and $\pi_t^Y = 0$.

Although e ranges from -1 to 1, it cannot assume the extreme values in its range if either $\pi_t^X > 0$ or $\pi_t^Y > 0$. In particular, the range of e is restricted whenever $I \neq J$, since one of π_t^X or π_t^Y is necessarily nonzero in that case. Moreover, the magnitude of e is less than one for (population) tables that exhibit weak perfect correlation. Thus, while d can be regarded as a measure of "weak" association, e is a measure that attains its extreme values only in the case of strict perfect correlation.

By the argument of Somers (1968), Wilson (1974) provides a "proportional-reduction-in-predictive-error" interpretation for e. Wilson further shows that $(e / \tau_b)^2$ is a decreasing function of the probability of pairs tied on one variable but not the other. It can be argued, therefore, that e is more sensitive to the degree to which the population clusters about the diagonal than is τ_b.

The maximum likelihood estimator of e under the multinomial sampling model is

$$\hat{e} = \frac{C - D}{C + D + T_X + T_Y}$$

where C, D, T_X, and T_Y are given, respectively, by equations 5.18, 5.22, 5.25, and 5.26. It is evident from equations 5.24 and 5.27 that

$$\hat{e} = \frac{2(C - D)}{n^2 - \sum_{i=1}^{I} \sum_{j=1}^{J} n_{ij}^2}$$

Statements about the properties of e and its relation to other measures contained in the preceding three paragraphs follow verbatim for e.

Like other closely related measures, $\hat{e}$ is asymptotically normal under the multinomial sampling model. the expected value of $\hat{e}$ is e. A formula for the variance of $\hat{e}$ has not been published. However, an estimate can be obtained from a formula given by Quade (1974: 392). By using only pairs of observations that are "relevant" to its definition, Quade's formula can be used to compute variance estimates for a large number of measures. All pairs that are not tied on both X and Y are relevant for computations involving e. When e = 0, the estimated variance of e becomes

$$\hat{\sigma}^2_\infty(\hat{e}) = \frac{4 \sum\limits_{i=1}^{I} \sum\limits_{j=1}^{J} n_{ij}(C_{ij} - D_{ij})^2 - \frac{4}{n}(C - D)^2}{\left(n^2 - \sum\limits_{i=1}^{I} \sum\limits_{j=1}^{J} n_{ij}^2\right)^2} \qquad [5.56]$$

Of course, equation 5.56 is appropriate only for testing the hypothesis e = 0.

Example 4 (continued). From Table 4, we see that

$$\sum_{i=1}^{I} \sum_{j=1}^{J} n_{ij}^2 = 70^2 + 85^2 + \ldots + 100^2 = 46{,}416$$

and, therefore,

$$\hat{e} = \frac{2(C - D)}{n^2 - \sum\limits_{i=1}^{I} \sum\limits_{j=1}^{J} n_{ij}^2} = \frac{73{,}280}{247{,}348} = 0.296$$

Notice that $\hat{e}$ is less than each of the other estimators to which it is related.

Wilson's 1974 paper is definitive for the measure e. A supplementary discussion, with examples, is given by Reynolds (1977a).

SUMMARY

It is worthwhile at this point to summarize the relationships among τ and its progeny. Analogous statements hold for the corresponding estimators.

(1) $d_{Y \cdot X} = d_{X \cdot Y} = \tau_b$ if, and only if, $\pi_t^X = \pi_t^Y$

(2) $\gamma = d_{Y \cdot X}$ if, and only if, $\pi_t^Y = 0$

   $\gamma = d_{X \cdot Y}$ if, and only if, $\pi_t^X = 0$

(3) $\tau_b = e$ if, and only if, $\pi_t^X = \pi_t^Y = 0$

If (3) holds, then all five of the measures τ_b, γ, $d_{Y \cdot X}$, $d_{X \cdot Y}$, and e are equal. Furthermore,

(4) if $\pi_t^X = \pi_t^Y = \pi_t^{XY} = 0$, than all five of these measures equal τ,

where $\tau = \pi_c - \pi_d$ is the measure originally defined for continuous populations. The sampling theory given in this chapter is inappropriate if (4) holds.

It has already been noted that

$$\tau_b^2 = d_{X \cdot Y} \times d_{Y \cdot X}$$

and it is easy enough to verify that

$$\frac{1}{\gamma} = \frac{1}{d_{X \cdot Y}} + \frac{1}{d_{Y \cdot X}} - \frac{1}{e}$$

Thus, τ_b and γ can easily be determined from $d_{X \cdot Y}$, $d_{Y \cdot X}$, and e. Wilson (1974: 338) argues that these three measures be taken as a "standard set" because each has a reasonable interpretation and because the "asymmetric and strict hypotheses seem to be of greatest substantive interest."

Comments concerning the numerical stability of these estimators in selected sampling situations are given in the next chapter.

Other Measures

Versions of Pearson's product-moment correlation coefficient and Spearman's rank correlation coefficient which are suitable for ordinal data have been published. The product-moment correlation coefficient is calculated from category scores by means of equation 4.9, and the rank correlation coefficient is computed from equation 4.30 using the ranks of category scores. Because these measures are less frequently used than those related to Kendall's tau, their properties are not considered here. The interested reader is referred to Brown and Benedetti (1977) for the correct variance formulas to use with these measures under the multinomial sampling model.

6. CHOOSING AN APPROPRIATE MEASURE

A large number of measures have been discussed in this monograph. With so many measures available, it is not always easy to select a suitable one. Nevertheless, the investigator can reduce the number of alternatives by focusing his or her attention on measures that have properties he or she considers important.

It is desirable to have a measure with a meaningful interpretation. Efforts have been made to give an interpretation for each estimator in terms of some meaningful population parameter or property. It is difficult to interpret measures based on the chi-square statistic and the various measures of the rank correlation coefficient, especially those that result from "norming" some other measure to give it a "nice" range. Generally speaking, the other measures considered have sensible interpretations.

Aside from the question of interpretation, guidelines for selecting an appropriate measure involve the nature and source of the data and the intended use of the measure. One must know whether the data are nominal, ordinal, or continuous in order to choose the correct class of measures. One must know why the measure is being computed in order to select a suitable measure from this class. It matters, for example, whether one is trying to predict, to measure agreement, or to establish association.

The following questions should prove helpful to someone faced with the task of selecting an appropriate measure.

(1) *Are the data nominal?* Measures for nominal data should not depend on category order. Choosing a measure that treats the order of category labels as meaningful when it is not can lead to completely erroneous conclusions.

(2) *Are the data continuous?* The choice in this case depends on what we can assume about the data. If the data are normally distributed, then ρ is the best choice. Otherwise, τ, or even ρ_s, may be a better choice.

The effect of ties should be considered, especially when it comes to choosing among the various measures of Spearman's rank correlation coefficient or Kendall's τ. To some extent, the choice depends on what one is trying to measure: If one is concerned with agreement between two judges, for example, then ρ_b and τ_b are recommended over their counterparts.

(3) *Are the data ordinal?* A good measure for ordinal data should depend on category order because information is lost if the order of the categories is ignored. Information is also lost when the range of a pair of continuous variables is categorized. A "stable" measure is desirable in this case because the loss of information increases as the number of categories decreases. A measure is stable to the extent that its value computed for the cross-classification is similar to that of the "associated measure for ungrouped data computed from the underlying continuous distribution" (Agresti, 1976: 49). Agresti has studied the stability of selected measures, including γ, τ_b, and τ_c, when the underlying bivariate distribution is normal. He concludes that none of the measures is very

stable when the number of categories is small. The Goodman-Kruskal γ is particularly unstable, while τ_b generally fares better than do the other measures. The stability of all measures considered by Agresti improves as ρ decreases.

It is best to avoid using ordinal data to make inferences about an underlying continuous population. If the original data are unavailable, it helps somewhat to assign category labels that are scalar, rather than merely ordinal.

(4) *Is the measure being computed to establish correlation, to measure agreement, or to make predictions, i.e., to establish a cause-effect relationship?* Any measure that treats the two variables symmetrically can be used to measure correlation. Asymmetric measures, such as the Goodman-Kruskal measures or Somers's d, should be used for prediction. If one is interested in how two variables or judges agree, then a suitable measure of agreement should be chosen.

(5) *Is the measure being used to make inferences?* The answer to this question is usually "yes." The ability to make statistical inferences about a measure depends on knowing the sampling distribution of its estimator. Nearly all estimators considered have sampling distributions that are approximately normal for large samples, so the problem becomes one of choosing the correct variance estimate. Under the multinomial model, the correct estimate of variance for testing the hypothesis of independence differs from the estimate to be used for constructing confidence intervals. The nature of the inference dictates the choice.

A study by Brown and Benedetti (1977) emphasizes the importance of using correct variance estimates. The authors have studied the empirical behavior of several measures "in a hypothesis testing situation where the underlying distribution is multinomial" (p. 309) for a variety of hypothetical contingency tables. Three estimates of asymptotic variance are considered: (a) one that is correct when the underlying variables are continuous, (b) one that is correct when the underlying distribution is multinomial, and (c) the modification of (b) that is suitable for testing the hypothesis of independence. The authors conclude that (c) is more reliable than (b) for testing for independence unless sample sizes are large. More important, they conclude that variance estimates computed for continuous populations are not good estimates of their discrete analogues, even for large samples, and therefore should not be used in a multinomial context.

(6) *Is the measure sensitive to marginal totals?* If so, differences between sample marginal probabilities and corresponding population proportions could result in fallacious inferences because the sampling values of the measure may not be representative of its population value. In particular, values of a measure computed from two different samples and/or populations cannot be compared if the measure depends upon marginal totals. Goodman and Kruskal (1954) give an example that shows how inferences can be distorted when tables with different marginal totals are compared. At best, such comparisons can be made only after sample marginals have been "standardized" in some fashion.

Nearly all measures for discrete data are sensitive to changes in marginal totals.

(7) *For what type of association does a measure assume its extreme values?* Some measures assume their extreme values in cases of weak perfect association, others in cases of implicit perfect association, and still others only in the case of strict perfect association. All other things being equal, an investigator should perhaps choose a measure that can assume its extreme values for the type of association that he or she considers most important.

7. CORRELATION AND CAUSATION

It is appropriate to conclude this monograph on a note of caution. When two variables have been shown to be correlated, it is indeed tempting to infer a cause-and-effect relationship between them. Most measures, however, treat the variables symmetrically (the value of the measure remains the same if the roles of the variables are interchanged), and such measures tell us nothing about causality. More sophisticated models are required to establish causality than are needed to merely identify association.

The chi-square statistic in equation 2.2 is symmetric in the sense described, and will be used to illustrate the point being made. Mann et al. (1975) conducted a study to test the theory that smoking causes myocardial infarction (heart attack) in women. In Table 6, a total of 216 patients are classified according to smoking habits (smoker, nonsmoker) and whether or not they had experienced myocardial infarction.

For these data, the statistic X^2 has the value

$$X^2 = \frac{216 (14 \cdot 83 - 45 \cdot 74)^2}{59 \cdot 157 \cdot 88 \cdot 128} = 9.73$$

TABLE 6
Classification of 216 Woman Patients According to Incidence
of Myocardial Infarction and Smoking Habits

| | | Myocardial Infarction | | |
		Yes	No	Totals
Smoker	Yes	45	83	128
	No	14	74	88
	Totals	59	157	216

SOURCE: Mann et al. (1975).

It is safe to conclude that the two factors are related, since the probability that $\dot{X}^2$ exceeds 9.73 is less than 0.01 if they are independent.

Showing that a relationship exists between smoking habits and myocardial infarction does not establish cause and effect. On the basis of the analysis presented here, it is equally as valid to conclude that heart attacks cause smoking as vice versa!

The reader interested in cause-effect modeling is referred to Fienberg (1980), Reynolds (1977a, 1977b) or Haberman (1978, 1979) for recent work on the important class of loglinear models.

NOTES

1. Technically, the multinomial distribution is the correct model for sampling with replacement. If sampling is without replacement, the correct model involves the hypergeometric distribution. In practice, differences between the two distributions are negligible if the population is large and the sample small enough relative to the population size. It makes little difference, for example, if a sample of size 25 is selected with or without replacement from the senior class at a large university.

2. Note that two different approximations have been discussed in this section. The binomial distribution can be used to approximate the hypergeometric distribution if the population is large in comparison with the sample size. The normal distribution can be used to approximate the binomial distribution if, in addition, the sample is large.

3. Table 1 exhibits IJ cells defined jointly by the variables X and Y. Here, the IJ cells are the k categories of the previous section, and the variables N_{ij} are the multinomial variables $X_1, \ldots, X_k$.

Wasserman © 1982, Los Angeles Times Syndicate. Reprinted with permission.

4. Two variables that exhibit this degree of association are said to be *perfectly associated* by some authors (see Reynolds, 1977b: 15-16, for example). In square tables (I = J), where each value of one variable is uniquely associated with a value of the other, the relationship is termed *strict*. When I ≠ J, the relationship is described as *implicit*.

5. The authors' four papers on measures of association, which originally appeared in 1954, 1959, 1963, and 1972, are presented here in book form. References to a specific paper cite the original date of publication.

6. The product multinomial model results when the rows (or columns) of the table are independent samples from two (possibly) different populations. With only two categories per row (or column), the product multinomial model becomes the product binomial model. For example, suppose we are interested in comparing the numbers of male and female faculty members at the various academic ranks. If the male and female faculty members are sampled independently, the product multinomial model is appropriate. This is in contrast to the case in which the entire faculty is sampled as a single population and the same members are then cross-classified according to academic rank and sex.

7. See the next two chapters for definitions of measures that have not previously been discussed.

8. If one cell of a fourfold table is zero, the variables are said to exhibit *weak* perfect association by some authors (see Reynolds, 1977b: 15-16, for example). The two variables are said to exhibit *strict* perfect association if two cells not in the same row or column contain zero. Thus, $|\rho| = 1$ only if A and B are strictly associated, while $|Q| = 1$ in both cases.

9. The covariance between two random variables X and Y is defined to be Cov (X, Y) = $\sigma(X, Y) = E[(X - \mu_X) (Y - \mu_Y)]$.

10. When sampling from a bivariate normal population, this hypothesis is equivalent to H_o: X and Y are independent.

11. If an increase in X always corresponds to an increase in Y, or if an increase in X always corresponds to a decrease in Y, then X and Y are monotonically related.

12. For more details, see the discussion of τ_c in the section on Measures Related to Kendall's τ_b. In the terminology of contingency tables, this is the case of strict perfect concordance.

13. It is more convenient to work with counts than with actual sample probabilities.

14. Thus, $|\tau_b| = 1$ for tables that exhibit strict perfect correlation, while $|\tau| < 1$ in other cases.

15. When $\pi_d = 0$, two variables X and Y are said to exhibit *weak perfect positive correlation*. Likewise, they are said to exhibit *weak perfect negative correlation* when $\pi_c = 0$. Similar statements can be made for samples, provided π_d and π_c are replaced by D and C, respectively.

REFERENCES

AGRESTI, A. (1976) "The effect of category choice on some ordinal measures of association." Journal of the American Statistical Association 71: 49-55.

ANDERSON, T. W. (1958) An Introduction to Multivariate Statistical Analysis. New York: John Wiley.

92

BERGESON, A. J. (1977) "Political witch hunts: the sacred and subversive in cross-national perspective." American Sociological Review 42: 220-233.

BISHOP, Y.M.M., S. E. FIENBERG, and P. W. HOLLAND (1975) Discrete Multivariate Analysis: Theory and Practice. Cambridge, MA: MIT Press.

BLALOCK, H. M. (1972) Social Statistics. New York: McGraw-Hill.

BROWN, M. B. [ed.] (1977) BMDP-77: Biomedical Computer Programs, P Series. Berkeley: University of California Press.

——— and J. K. BENEDETTI (1977) "Sampling behavior of tests for correlation in two-way contingency tables." Journal of the American Statistical Association 72: 309-315.

COHEN, J. (1968) "Weighted kappa: nominal scale agreement with provision for scaled disagreement or partial credit." Psychological Bulletin 70: 213-220.

——— (1960) "A coefficient of agreement for nominal scales." Educational and Psychological Measurement 20: 37-46.

COLEMAN, J. S. (1966) "Measuring concordance in attitudes." Baltimore: Johns Hopkins University, Department of Social Relations. (unpublished)

CONOVER, W. J. (1980) Practical Nonparametric Statistics. New York: John Wiley.

CRAMER, H. (1946) Mathematical Methods of Statistics. Princeton, NJ: Princeton University Press.

FIENBERG, S. E. (1980) The Analysis of Cross-Classified Categorical Data. Cambridge, MA: MIT Press.

FISHER, R. A. (1921) "On the 'probable error' of a coefficient of correlation deduced from a small sample." Metron 1, 4: 3-32.

——— (1915) "Frequency distribution of the values of the correlation coefficient in samples from an indefinitely large population." Biometrika 10: 507-521.

FLEISS, J. L. (1971) "Measuring nominal scale agreement among many raters." Psychological Bulletin 76: 378-382.

——— J. COHEN, and B. S. EVERITT (1969) "Large sample standard errors of kappa and weighted kappa." Psychological Bulletin 72: 323-327.

GIBBONS, J. D. (1971) Nonparametric Statistical Inference. New York: McGraw-Hill.

GINI, C. (1912) "Variabilita e mutabilita contributo allo studio delle distribuzioni; relazione statische," in Studie Economico-Guiridici della R. Universita di Cagliari.

GOODMAN, L. A. and W. H. KRUSKAL (1980) Measures of Association for Cross-Classifications. Springer Series in Statistics, Vol. 1. New York: Springer-Verlag.

——— (1972) "Measures of association for cross-classifications, IV: simplification of asymptotic variances." Journal of the American Statistical Association 67: 415-421.

——— (1963) "Measures of association for cross-classification, III: Approximate sampling theory." Journal of the American Statistical Association 58: 310-364.

——— (1959) "Measures of association for cross-classifications, II: further discussion and references." Journal of the American Statistical Association 54: 123-163.

——— (1954) "Measures of association for cross-classifications. Journal of the American Statistical Association 49: 732-764.

GUTTMAN, L. (1941) "An outline of the statistical theory of prediction," pp. 253-318 in P. Horst et al. (eds.) The Prediction of Personal Adjustment. Bulletin 48. New York: Social Science Research Council.

HABERMAN, S. J. (1979) Analysis of Qualitative Data, Vol. II. New York: Academic.
——— (1978) Analysis of Qualitative Data, Vol. I. New York: Academic.
HAYS, W. L. (1963) Statistics for Psychologists. New York: Holt, Rinehart & Winston.
HOEFFDING, W. (1948) "A class of statistics with asymptotically normal distribution." Annals of Mathematical Statistics 19: 293-325.
KENDALL, M. G. (1970) Rank Correlation Methods. London: Griffin.
——— and A. STUART (1973) The Advanced Theory of Statistics, Vol. II. New York: Hafner.
KRUSKAL, W. H. (1958) "Ordinal measures of association." Journal of the American Statistical Association 53: 814-861.
KUKLINSKI, J. H. and D. M. WEST (1981) "Economic expectations and voting behavior in United States House and Senate elections." American Political Science Review 75: 436-447.
LEIK, R. K. and W. R. GROVE (1971) "Integrated approach to measuring association," pp. 279-301 in H. L. Costner (ed.) Sociological Methodology. San Francisco: Jossey-Bass.
LIGHT, R. J. (1971) "Measures of response agreement for qualitiative data: some generalizations and alternatives." Psychological Bulletin 76: 365-377.
——— (1969) "Analysis of variance for categorical data, with application to agreement and association." Ph.D. dissertation, Department of Statistics, Harvard University.
——— and B. H. MARGOLIN (1971) "An analysis of variance for categorical data." Journal of the American Statistical Association 66: 534-544.
MANN, J. I., M. P. VESSEY, M. THOROGOOD, and R. DOLL (1975) "Myocardial infarction in young women with special reference to oral contraceptive practice." British Medical Journal 2: 241-245.
MARGOLIN, B. H. and R. J. LIGHT (1974) "An analysis of variance for categorical data, II: small sample comparisons with chi-square and other competitors." Journal of the American Statistical Association 69: 755-764.
MORRISON, D. F. (1976) Multivariate Statistical Methods. New York: McGraw-Hill.
NIE, N. H., C. H. HULL, J. G. JENKINS, K. STEINBRENNER, and D. H. BENT (1975) Statistical Package for the Social Sciences. New York: McGraw-Hill.
NOETHER, G. E. (1967) Elements of Nonparametric Statistics. New York: John Wiley.
OWEN, D. B. (1962) Handbook of Statistical Tables. Reading, MA: Addison-Wesley.
PEARSON, K. (1948) [1904] "Mathematical contributions to the theory of evolution, XIII. on the theory of contingency and its relation to association and normal correlation." Draper's Co. Res. Mem. Biometric. Ser. 1. Reprinted in Karl Pearson's Early Papers. Cambridge: Cambridge University Press.
PEARSON, K. (1896) "Mathematical contributions to the theory of evolution, III. Regression, heredity, and panmixia." Philosophical Transcriptions of the Royal Society A 187: 253-318.
QUADE, D. (1974) "Nonparametric partial correlation," pp. 369-398 in H. M. Blalock, Jr. (ed.) Measurement in the Social Sciences. Chicago: Aldine-Atherton.
REYNOLDS, H. T. (1977a) The Analysis of Cross-Classifications. New York: Free Press.
——— (1977b) Analysis of Nominal Data. Sage University Papers series on Quantitative Applications in the Social Sciences, 07-007. Beverly Hills, CA: Sage.
SAKODA, J. M. (1977) "Measures of association for multivariate contingency tables," pp. 777-780 in Social Statistics Section Proceedings for the American Statistical Association.

SIEGEL, S. (1956) Nonparametric Statistics for the Behavioral Sciences. New York: McGraw-Hill.

SNEDECOR, G. W. and W. G. COCHRAN (1967) Statistical Methods. Ames: Iowa State University Press.

SOMERS, R. H. (1968) "On the measurement of association." American Sociological Review 33: 291-292.

——— (1962a) "A new asymmetric measure of association for ordinal variables." American Sociological Review 27: 799-811.

——— (1962b) "A similarity between Goodman and Kruskal's tau and Kendall's tau, with a partial interpretation of the latter." Journal of the American Statistical Association 57: 804-812.

STUART, A. (1963) "Calculation of Spearman's rho for ordered two-way classifications." American Statistician 17, 4: 23-24.

——— (1953) "The estimation and comparison of strengths of association in contingency tables." Biometrika 40: 105-110.

SPEARMAN, C. (1904) "The proof and measurement of association between two things." American Journal of Psychology 15: 72-101.

TSCHUPROW, A. A. (1918/1919/1921) "On the mathematical expectation of the moments of frequency distributions." Biometrika 12/13: 140-169, 185-210, 283.

WILSON, T. P. (1974) "Measures of association for bivariate ordinal hypotheses," pp. 327-342 in H. M. Blalock, Jr. (ed.) Measurement in the Social Sciences. Chicago: Aldine-Atherton.

——— (1969) "A proportional-reduction-in-error interpretation for Kendall's tau-b." Social Forces 47: 340-342.

YULE, G. U. (1912) "On the methods of measuring association between two attributes." Journal of the Royal Statistical Society 75: 579-642.

——— (1900) "On the association of attributes in statistics." Philosophical Transcriptions of the Royal Society A194: 257-319.

ALBERT M. LIEBETRAU is a Senior Research Scientist in the Probabilistic Modeling Group at the Battelle Pacific Northwest Laboratory in Richland, Washington. He holds degrees from the University of Wisconsin and Oregon State University. After receiving his Ph.D. in statistics from the University of Michigan, Dr. Liebetrau joined the faculty of the Johns Hopkins University. Since coming to Battelle in 1983, he has concentrated on the development and application of probabilistic systems performance models. He has extensive consulting experience, and his publications include articles in the Journal of Applied Probability, *the* Journal of the Royal Statistical Society (Series B), Communications in Statistics, Geographical Analysis, *and* Water Resources Research. *The statistical methods that he has developed for the treatment of volume calibration and measurement data are internationally recognized. He currently represents the United States as a member of the Probabilistic Systems Assessment Codes Users Group of the OECD Nuclear Energy Agency.*